ONE LIFE

ONE LIFE

MEGAN RAPINOE

WITH EMMA BROCKES

RANDOM HOUSE
LARGE PRINT

All photographs from the author's collection.

Cover photograph: Jody Rogac

The Library of Congress has established a
Cataloging-in-Publication record for this title.

ISBN: 978-0-593-29558-8

www.penguinrandomhouse.com/
large-print-format-books

FIRST LARGE PRINT EDITION

Printed in the United States of America

10 9 8 7 6 5 4 3 2 1

This Large Print edition published in accord
with the standards of the N.A.V.H.

For Sue,
who put me back together and made me
invincible. I can only hope to love you
the same way.

And Mammers,
you're the center of the universe for all of us, and
the OG of unsolicited advice.

And Dad,
for your quiet strength and infectious smile,
and unsolicited advice.

And Rachy,
forever my wombmate and partner in crime,
and unsolicited advice.

And Brian,
forever my inspiration, and for your
unsolicited advice.

And Jenny,
for your loving heart, and unsolicited advice.

And Michael,
for your big bear heart, and unsolicited advice.

And CeCé,
for your infinite kindness,
and unsolicited advice.

And Austin,
you are our light and forever our Doodlebop,
and even you give unsolicited advice.

Tell me, what is it you plan to do with your one wild and precious life?

—Mary Oliver, "The Summer Day"

CONTENTS

ONE LIFE

PROLOGUE

I want to start by saying something about the purpose of this book. A frequent criticism of people who have a lot of media attention is that they're using the spotlight to leverage themselves and hijack the moment. You become famous and you run with it. You make a commercial, you put out a perfume, you cash in with a book or reality show. I am **totally** cashing in to capitalize on the moment. I'm just doing it for what I hope are reasons that aren't exclusively seedy. In the pages that follow, you will read about my childhood in Northern California; my twin sister, Rachael; my hilarious mom and wacky dad; as well as my highs and lows with the US women's national soccer team. But while I have your attention, I also want to discuss issues that are important to me and have nothing to do with sports or my family.

As a child, I was small for my age. I was shy and let my sister speak for me. I didn't always fit in. And while I was a natural athlete from the get-go—Rachael and I could both do double Dutch in kindergarten—for a while, I wasn't totally sure of myself. Not until I was eighteen and in college did I even realize I was gay, for god's sake, something that, given how completely obvious it was in hindsight, I'm still pissed at my family for not pointing out sooner.

Like almost everyone in my hometown, my family was socially and politically conservative, although we weren't an overtly political household. The lessons I learned growing up had to do with standing up to bullies and doing the right thing, part of which, my parents said, meant acknowledging how lucky we were. There were lots of kids in our family and we didn't have much money, but we grew up in a safe, loving environment where all our needs were met. On top of that, my twin and I were cute, good at sports, and popular at school. We had it incredibly easy.

We were also white. This might seem like stating the obvious, but I honestly think many white people don't realize they are wandering around with a four-hundred-year baked-in advantage. I know I didn't. After college, I could talk about environmental and women's rights, and as I got older I spoke more about LGBTQ rights and pay equity. But it took me longer to piece together an understanding of how power and politics work beneath the surface and beyond my immediate experience. The very fact that I'm addressing you now, in a book I received lots of money for and began writing at the end of a year when I won every possible award, isn't simply because I'm a good soccer player or, as athletes love to say, because I worked really hard. (You know who else works hard? Everyone.)

The platform I've been given is a result of other aspects of my life, including the way I look, what I represent, and the associations that come with the sport I play. A small, white, female soccer player—even a lesbian one with a loud voice and pink hair—lands differently in the press than, say, a six-foot-four-inch black football player with an Afro.

It took me a while to get here. Speaking up can be embarrassing. Walking into a room to ask for more money can be super awkward, as can calling people out for being racist. People get angry. They get angry even when you don't say anything to them personally. It's amazing to see what makes people go off, particularly when a woman is doing the speaking. As a professional female athlete I can't—or I'm not supposed to—curse in public, talk too much about politics, wild out after winning, suggest I might be really good at what I do, or admit to being interested in money. Men play sports because they love it and want to get rich; women are there for the purity of the game.

I'm not supposed to squander my celebrity, either. Judging by my fellow athletes, the rule of thumb is that once you have wealth and fame, you must do everything you can to hang on to them. I've made a lot of mistakes in the past four years. I'm not exactly a forward thinker. I didn't map out what might happen if I took various political stands, like the tanking of my business or strangers from Florida calling my parents to ask them where they went wrong with me.

But I have always understood that once you have a tiny bit of power, space, or control, you should do everything you can to share it. I don't think you need a big platform to do this. It can be as simple as pushing back against a bigoted remark when you don't belong to the group being targeted. It can be taking time to think about Trayvon Martin, Sandra Bland, Eric Garner, Philando Castile, Walter Scott, Tamir Rice, Michael Brown, and countless others, and to consider why, when I say those names in public, I continue to be invited to the party when others don't. Sometimes, what I've said or done has caused a big fuss. But given the breaks I've had, speaking out seems like the least I can fucking do.

And here's the thing: the more you stand up for others, the easier it is to stand up for yourself. I love playing soccer. It's the only job I've ever had. I want to play and I want to win, but given the amount my team and I **do** win—given, as the US Soccer Federation likes to put it, the market realities—I also want to buy a gold Rolex and I don't think it's outrageous to say that. Equally, I don't think it's outrageous to say that while I'm grateful for my talent and other accidents of birth, I'm not grateful to the people making money from me and my teammates. I think they should be grateful to **us**.

In 2019, after my team won the World Cup for the second time, we played a bunch of exhibition games around the country. It was a victory lap of sorts, but I got a bigger kick out of another tour I went on that year, talking to people at companies, charities, schools, and colleges, and on panels with other feminists and social justice campaigners. I talked about paying men and women equally, and about calling out sexism, racism, and homophobia. I talked about the perceived risks of activism and also the joys, the fact that caring is cool and lowering the ladder can raise your own game. In soccer, scoring a goal and hearing fifty thousand people scream your name is awesome, but I take a lot of pride in my assists, too; setting someone else up to score—being the opportunity maker—is just as important, if not more.

I'm not the best soccer player in the world. I'm pretty high up there, but that's where my expertise ends. Beyond that, I don't know anything that anyone else doesn't know and I'm not doing anything that others can't do. We all have the same resource, our one precious life, made up of the decisions we make every day. Here, I'm telling the story of how I made my decisions, from the choice I made when I kicked that first ball to the one I made in 2016 that risked bringing my career crashing down. In telling it, I hope I'm also asking a question: What are you going to do?

INTRODUCTION

STAND UP

I was on the team bus driving through the suburbs of Chicago when I picked up a call from my agent. It was September 2016, and my team, FC Seattle Reign, had just played the Chicago Red Stars in one of the last games of the season. That wasn't why my agent was calling. Dan Levy had represented me for almost ten years and we'd been through a few things together. Five years earlier, he'd been a big part of the discussion around my decision to come out as the first, and for a long time practically the only, gay player on the US Women's National Team—which is hilarious given the number of gays on the team—and he'd seen me through injuries and disappointments without losing his cool. Now he sounded concerned. "This is blowing up," he said.

The actual game that night had been nothing special. Chicago, like New York and Los Angeles, isn't a soccer town, for reasons no one can quite put their finger on. You might get people out for a national team game, but no way are they turning up on a random Sunday night in September for a league match. We'd played to a small crowd of three thousand people and the score had been a lackluster 2–2. But at the press conference afterward, the first question out of the gate had little to do with the game itself: Had I intended to kneel during the national anthem, and if so, why?

I had anticipated being asked this question, of course. The decision to kneel wasn't one I'd made lightly. At the same time, I hadn't given much thought to how it might be received. In trivial contexts, I can be impulsive—the kind of person who dyes their hair pink the night before a huge tournament, for example—but it wasn't that. If I didn't rehearse outcomes before kneeling, it's because kneeling, to me, felt more like an imperative than a choice. Any risk assessment I did wasn't premised on how my actions might land, but on calculating the risk—huge, societal, unignorable, in my view—of doing nothing.

Still, I wasn't expecting much of a backlash. Compared to football or baseball, soccer has a relatively low profile in this country, particularly at the league level. The nine teams in the National

Women's Soccer League are very competitive, but they don't exactly dominate the sports pages. In the fall of 2016, even the national team—one of the most successful sports teams of all time—wasn't riding especially high. A month earlier, we'd been eliminated from of the Rio Olympics in the quarterfinals, our worst result in an international tournament for years. I was personally off form, in the final stages of recovering from a knee injury. And the soccer season was about to end.

I was also a woman athlete. At thirty-one, I was a veteran of two World Cups and two Olympic Games, with a history of mouthing off at least as long as my playing record. Still, it seemed fair to assume that when it came to talking about politics, my voice would carry less weight than a man's. Earlier that year, when members of three WNBA basketball teams had worn T-shirts emblazoned with BLACK LIVES MATTER, it had triggered a flurry of interest before dying down. By contrast, when Colin Kaepernick, quarterback for the 49ers, had knelt before a game in San Diego a week earlier, the response had been swift and engulfing.

I had seen the footage of Colin kneeling. It was impossible to avoid. We were in an election year, and all summer the news had been dominated by stories of unarmed black Americans dying in police custody. Black Lives Matter had become increasingly visible. For a while, you couldn't open **The New York Times** without reading about the disparity between the way black and white Americans were treated by the criminal justice system and our society at large. When Colin knelt, it had seemed to me a perfectly logical response to what felt like a state of emergency. "I am not going to stand up to show pride in a flag for a country that oppresses black people and people of color," he said, and the invitation—surely everyone else heard it, too?—was clear.

The morning after I knelt in Chicago, a quick glance at my social media feeds confirmed the scale of my misapprehension. Dan's heads-up the night before had been a tiny taste of what was to come: people were **mad**. Whoa, were they pissed. When I was younger, I had labored under the delusion that dating men might be a part of my future. This felt like a bigger miscalculation.

It wasn't just the volume of outrage; it was the sheer hysterical pitch of it. I had been expecting a few chin-stroking editorials or a hashtag at most. Instead there were death threats, threats of violence, and horrible language, most of them sent to Dan and his fellow agents, often accompanied by a prim note asking if they'd mind forwarding the message on to me. A guy identifying himself as a former fan said he was thinking of burning my shirt. I was called every name under the sun. As the photo of me kneeling spread across the internet, right-wing blog posts sprung up calling for me to be axed from the team, and I was a talking point on Fox News. I was totally blindsided.

I called my parents in Redding. It's a small town in Northern California, a formerly prosperous outpost of the logging industry, now at the tail end of a long, slow economic decline. With the exception of Rachael, most of the rest of my family—parents, siblings, aunts, uncles, nephews, nieces—still live in the area and, my parents told me that morning, in between worrying about me, reeling at the scale of the coverage, and being mad that I hadn't given them advance notice, they were all having to deal with the reactions of their conservative neighbors.

One by one my siblings started to check in. CeCé, who I think of as my oldest sister but is actually my youngest aunt on my mother's side and by far the sweetest of us all, called to make sure I was OK. My oldest sister, Jenny, who with the best will in the world no one would describe as sweet, called in a state of alarm to tell me she was having to unfriend coworkers on Facebook after they kept posting links to articles that trashed me. Rachael was on a hiking holiday in the Swiss Alps. After three days in the mountains without wi-fi, she reached a village, turned on her phone, and watched as it practically vibrated off the table with messages—mostly from friends asking, "Have you seen what Megan's done?!" She hadn't, but was soon up to speed. We own a business together, Rapinoe SC, which runs soccer clinics for kids across the country, and through the company's website, hate mail was piling up in her in-box, along with cancellations for forthcoming clinics. When she called me, she barely needed the aid of a satellite to be heard. "What the hell is going on?" she yelled.

I had a tough time coming up with an answer. As the team and I packed up in Chicago and prepared to fly to our next game in DC, the noise intensified. I had been disrespectful to veterans, I was anti-American, I was politicizing sports in a way that ruined them for everyone else. I had long, reasoned responses to each of these accusations, but first, I was furiously indignant. So we don't think there's police brutality going on? We don't? OK. So that's what you're saying. You're saying all this stuff doesn't exist, and all these people's experiences—they're lying? The scale of the outrage seemed to me to underline the very problem we were addressing, which is that there is huge denial about race in this country, bolstered by white fragility.

Not all of the anger came from outside. My family rallied to my defense, as they always do, but that isn't to say everyone agreed with me. My dad and I hadn't seen eye to eye on politics for a while. Rachael, who totally approved of my politics, was still mad at me for not planning things out better, while other family members wondered aloud if kneeling was the best way to get my point across. The only person who, I imagined, might have been enjoying a straightforwardly positive response to what I'd done was my brother Brian. I hadn't spoken to Brian in a while, but one grimly amusing result of my kneeling was that it pushed him several places down the league table of Rapinoe sibling to have caused the most trouble.

There was one person I desperately wanted to talk to. Sue Bird was a star player on the national women's basketball team, who I had met at the Olympics in Rio that summer. After reconnecting briefly in Chicago, we had agreed not to meet up again until I'd returned to Seattle and broken up with my fiancée. I had never felt this way about anyone before, and in ordinary circumstances, it would have been enough drama to last me the year. Now, as the controversy around me raged on, Sue was the person I most wanted to be with and couldn't.

Not all the responses to my kneeling were bad. My Seattle teammates, while largely baffled by what I'd done, were also quietly supportive, as was my team coach, Laura Harvey, and Bill and

Teresa Predmore, two of the owners of the Seattle Reign. In the airport, on the street, and amid
the torrent of abusive messages online, strangers
came forward to offer encouragement. As tends
to happen, however, the negative stuff took up
the most space, and as journalists kept asking if
I planned on kneeling again, I found myself in a
familiar position. The quickest way to get me to
double down on something is to tell me I can't do
it. It didn't occur to me for a second that it might
not be my decision to make.

Three days after the game in Chicago, the
Seattle Reign played the Washington Spirit at
a stadium in Maryland. As I was changing, Laura
quietly came up and told me that the owner of
the Washington team had decided to play the national anthem while we were still in the locker
room, to deny me the possibility of kneeling.
"That is fucking wack-ass," I said, and burst into
laughter. It seemed cowardly and dishonest, the
worst possible way to deal with someone with
whom you disagree. It also signified the beginning of a new phase, in which strangers swearing
at me online was replaced by a worse phenomenon: people being polite to my face while trying
to defuse my actions behind my back.

By "people" I mean the US Soccer Federation.
Once they saw what was happening, they tried to

shut down my protest. The strangest thing about this was dealing with something people of color must feel all the time: the out-of-body experience of having one's basic reality denied. Every time I opened my mouth to talk about kneeling, or racial injustice, or police brutality, it was as if a chorus within the soccer world popped up to say: That isn't happening, and the real crime is you disturbing the peace by even suggesting it. In fact, those who disagreed seemed to be saying: Not only is your protest illegitimate, but the anger directed toward you isn't happening either, or at least people aren't angry for the reasons you specify. I couldn't get used to this. I understood that people were mad; I even understood, thanks to my dad's dalliances with right-wing views, that people can be manipulated into blaming the wrong people for their problems. What I couldn't understand was how anyone with half a brain or conscience could argue that there wasn't an issue here worth protesting, or that action soon taken against me by the Soccer Federation was anything but an attempt to quiet me down.

The beginning of the end came on a Thursday evening in mid-September. It was the first time since kneeling that I'd played with the national team, on a very different stage from that of a league game, with higher stakes and a bigger audience—around ten thousand that night, in the stadium in Columbus, Ohio. It was an international friendly against Thailand and, as always, we were the favorites, ranked number one in the world to Thailand's thirty-two. Before the game, Jill Ellis, the national coach, had been asked what she thought of my kneeling and said something vague about being "team first," which, while it wasn't a ringing endorsement, hadn't struck me as particularly ominous. In pleasant 70-degree weather, the anthem started to play. I dropped to one knee.

I didn't play the first half. In the second half, when I came in off the bench, a noise started to emanate from the crowd that, since it rose every time I received the ball and diminished every time I passed it, soon became unmistakable: boo-ing. Three days later, in a friendly against the Netherlands in Atlanta, it would be much, much louder. (It figures; it was the South.) But that game against Thailand was critical in terms of the effect I believe the booing had on my coach. For Jill, the sound coming from the bleachers that night in Ohio was, I suspect, her first real taste of what had been going on in the wake of my kneel-ing. From that moment on, my relationship with her was in serious trouble.

Tunnel vision is a prerequisite for most profes-sional athletes. Just as when you take a penalty kick in front of fifty thousand people—the am-bient cheering settles into white noise—it turns out that the sound of ten thousand people telling you to go fuck yourself can also blend into a solid mass possible to ignore. I wasn't disturbed by the booing that evening, nor during the game in Atlanta. If you want to be an asshole and boo social justice, I thought, go ahead, be my guest. But while we won 9–0 that night—a good result even by our standards—it would be my last celebration on the field for some time. After the game, US Soccer released a statement saying it expected players to stand for the anthem. The day after that, Jill told me she wasn't starting me in the game in Atlanta. A few weeks later, I was told by Jill not to dress for two national team games, guaranteeing I wouldn't set foot on the field, and with the exception of a training camp I attended in November, I wouldn't be invited to train with the team again that winter, or the following spring. In early 2017, the US Soccer Federation formally banned players from kneeling during the anthem.

This should have been the worst time of my life. I was in the wilderness with no team, no training camp, and no workable relationship with my coach. And while I was still technically a team member—Jill hadn't fired me, yet—what does that mean when you're not even invited to train, let alone to play? My career as a national team player was shattered. I was out in the cold with no obvious path of return. And yet, as my agents discussed the possibility that I might never play for my country again, I didn't feel despondent at all. I felt ignited. Everything in my life had been leading to this.

At the post-game press conference after I first knelt in Chicago, I hadn't rehearsed what I was going to say. I didn't need to. Still red-faced from playing, I said I had knelt in support of Colin and to start what I hoped was a more thoughtful conversation about race. It was a show of solidarity and, I said, a way to broaden the conversation about racial injustice to people who, to put it politely, might find me a less threatening messenger than Colin.

It was something else, too. I wasn't just familiar with the politics behind Colin's protest; I felt them, in my own way. "I know what it means to look at the flag and not have it protect all of your liberties," I said. "It was something small that I could do."

1

COUNTRY LIFE

Mrs. Walmart didn't like me. I was seven years old, dressed like a boy, and in a moment of rashness had stuck out my tongue at her. It wasn't my first offense; I'd had a few red cards for talking in class and a note had gone home to my parents. My mom knew I could be boisterous—there was no question about that—but she wasn't convinced I was the only party at fault. Mrs. Walmart was a crotchety teacher, and I was a whippersnapper, and so my mom volunteered to come in as a class parent. This way, she could keep an eye on me and assess whether I was being picked on by my teacher or was simply being obnoxious.

The latter was a definite possibility. I was an emotional kid in first grade, with no idea how to handle those emotions. A funny thing about twins is that they can switch personalities. You don't mean to; it just happens. One of you takes one position and the other, instinctively, will balance things out. In junior high, I would be the quiet one trailing in Rachael's wake, but in grade school it was the other way around. All through kindergarten (which our mom made us repeat, until she felt Rachael was ready to move up a grade), I'd answered for my sister in class and I was just as outspoken at home. Our grandpa had nicknames for us both at that age—I was Ma Barker to my sister's Sweet Muffin.

Part of my loudness was temperament, but there was definitely a practical side to it, too. We were a large, rambunctious family and you had to raise your voice or no one would hear you. By the time Rachael and I were born in 1985, our oldest brother, Michael, had moved out to live with his dad in San Diego, but that still left CeCé, who was fifteen and had been living with my parents since she was eleven; Jenny, eight; and five-year-old Brian; plus a series of extended family members who came and went over the years. Right after we were born, my mom's sister Melanie and her daughter, Aleta, lived with us for a while. When we were in high school, my grandpa Jack moved in. And much later, my parents took in Austin, Brian's son, and raised him from babyhood.

This is what my parents do—they look after

people. My mom, Denise, since forever—she is the second eldest of eight children and the oldest girl, with parents who were both alcoholics—and my dad, Jim, from the age of thirty, when he married my mom. She was twenty-three when they started dating and came with a lot of baggage: a bitter ex-husband, two young children, a dying mother out in Nevada, and a soon-to-be orphaned nine-year-old sister, who needed somewhere to live. It was a lot for a thirty-year-old bachelor to take on, particularly one who was struggling professionally. When my parents met, my dad had been living in San Diego for ten years and had worked as a commercial fisherman, a car salesman, the owner of a flatbed truck, and a rane operator. My mom, meanwhile, had been a waitress, a dental assistant, and a clerk at a shipping company, and at that point was mainly caring for her mom.

A lot of guys in my dad's shoes would have run for the hills. There was nothing in his background that prepared him for my mom's family, a huge Catholic clan—my mom has thirty-two first cousins, and that's just on her mom's side—that had lived through some pretty tough times. Her dad, who had been in the army, was verbally abusive and highly critical of his kids, and, at least toward the boys, sporadically violent. He was also serially unemployed. Growing up in San Bernardino, the family was frequently broke, and while my mom's mom was a coper, she was often put in the impossible position of trying to raise eight kids on a waitress's salary.

My dad, by contrast, was raised in a stable middle-class home by a stay-at-home mom and a firefighter dad. He had one brother, which is why, perhaps, he was so drawn to my mom's large family. Far from being alienated by the mess and the noise, my dad found it wonderfully warm and inviting. My parents have a lot in common—both moved to Southern California from other parts of the country as kids. Both had fathers who were veterans—my paternal grandfather had fought in France in the Second World War, and my mom's dad was a veteran of the Korean War, which, looking back, explained some of his behaviors. Long after the fact, my mom and her siblings realized he probably had undiagnosed PTSD.

Both my parents are easygoing, generous, hardworking people with a kooky sense of humor. But most of all, they place a high value on family. My mom never says no when someone needs a bed for the night; my dad is a shirt-off-his-back kind of guy. After the disappointment of Bill, my mom's first husband, who could be slightly too much like her dad for comfort, her siblings fell in love with my dad, and for a while the refrain when someone needed help in the family was "Call Jim!" After my parents married and had Brian, it seemed natural to them to move up to Redding, to be near my mom's sisters. A year after they moved they had Rachael and me.

Everyone assumes there is a special bond between twins and there is, although it's not quite the way people like to imagine. Rachael and I don't read each other's minds. And we don't really finish each other's sentences. Of all our siblings, we don't even look the most alike—I probably look more like Brian, or at least I did as a kid. Still, the twin relationship is unique. The very fact that I refer to myself as "we" a lot of the time is weird when you come to think of it. (We also call ourselves "wombmates"—sorry.) Rachael was the firstborn, and after she came out like clockwork, the doctors had a brief panic about how long I was taking. To get me out, they had to give me a mighty push; my mom's sister Wendy, who was there for the birth because our dad had the flu and couldn't be in the delivery room, likes to say the effects of that push are still being felt.

Having a twin is like having a mirror. Rachael is my built-in ally, my sounding board, the safety net I always know is 100 percent secure. For the first seven years of my life, before we were separated for first grade, she was barely out of my sight. And no matter how much we fought, when one of us was in trouble, the other always leapt to her defense. When we were toddlers, Rachael was put in her crib as punishment for touching a hot stove, and when my mom looked in on her a few moments later, there I was, lying on the floor, holding her hand through the bars like someone consoling a prisoner.

Our house was out in Palo Cedro, a tiny semirural community to the east of Redding, with stunning views of the mountains. I can be a bit dismissive of Redding these days. It's a town of ninety thousand people at the top of the Sacramento Valley, an annoying two-hour drive from the Sacramento airport, and—unless you're into tattoo parlors and breweries—with nothing much to do when you get there. The summers are too hot (when my mom was heavily pregnant with us, she waddled around in a 115-degree heat wave) and the winters too cold, and while it's beautiful country, with great outdoor sports and hiking, Redding itself is unremarkable. All the same, I love it. It's full of good people, most of whom I disagree with about politics, and it's still the place I think of as home.

And there's no question that, as a corner of the world to grow up in, it was amazing. Our house on Oak Meadow Road was typical of the properties in that area, a blue-painted, four-bedroom ranch, situated on three acres and set way back from the road. We had cats and dogs. Our neighbors had horses and sheep. There was a creek around the bend and an empty field across the street, all of which we were free to roam until dinnertime, when my mom would stand in the yard, put her two index fingers in the sides of her mouth, and whistle to call us back in.

We had freedom, with boundaries. (I once made the mistake of lying low and ignoring my mom's end-of-the-day whistle, something I never did again.) After endless games of hide-and-seek, laser tag, and hours spent catching crawdads in the creek with our cousin Stevie, we ran back to the house, where it was often my dad who made dinner. No one talked about "gender roles" in those days, at least not in Redding, but my parents, who both worked, were unusual in how they took care of the family. My dad did more outdoor stuff and my mom more indoor stuff, but overall they divided things pretty equally—my mom getting us up and ready for school in the morning; my dad, after a long day on the construction site, doing dinner, bath, and bedtime while my mom pulled a late shift at Jack's Grill.

One night a week, my dad would yell, "Rake-out!" to which we would all scream, "We hate rake-out!" "Rake-out" meant clearing out and eating all the leftovers from the fridge, and if we hated it, tough. There was no way my parents were going to throw away food and there was no way we could opt out of dinner. On the nights my mom hadn't already left for the restaurant, we'd sit around the table as a family. (I remember CeCé telling me she'd never had a TV dinner before she left for college and was so excited to try one.) Dinner was an important time, a chance for everyone to share details of their day, and to laugh and joke together.

We fought, too, of course. Especially in big families, everyone thinks they had it the hardest. My sister Jenny likes to remind me that when she and CeCé were small, our mom used to make them weed the yard—"even though Mom never planted anything!"—which, when Rachael and I came along, we were spared, to howls of "It isn't fair!" And I like to remind her of the time she was babysitting us when we were five, and she dragged me across the floor when I was being stubborn (read: kicking her shins), and accidentally popped one of my arms out of its socket, nearly depriving the United States of a future star winger. As the youngest in the family, Rachael and I got away with a lot based on cuteness and the fact that, long after infancy, we were still referred to as "the babies." But there were still bigger kids up the food chain who could boss us around.

I didn't mind being the youngest. Even as a child, I could give as good as I got. What I struggled with in early childhood was, oddly, not being bossed around, but being consoled. If I was angry, hurt, or upset, the last thing in the world

I wanted was for someone to witness my injury. I would scream and howl and run to my room, where I would stay until I had figured out how to calm down. Very occasionally, CeCé could tempt me out by knocking gently on the door and saying, "Meggy, are you OK?" But generally I didn't want consolation.

All kids cry. But the sheer rage I felt when I lost control of my emotions was something else. It's where my nickname Ma Barker came from, and even now I'm not sure what was going on. When Rachael was upset, she wanted to be soothed right away. But for me, the most embarrassing thing in the world was to lose my composure in front of people. These days, I'm almost impossible to embarrass, and I wonder if those early years of self-consciousness somehow acted as an inoculation. On some level, I understood I had to get a handle on myself and learn how to metabolize disappointment, frustration, and anger—all things that, twenty years later, I would encounter every day on the soccer field.

To other members of the family, of course, I was simply a pain in the ass. "Nise needs to get a handle on that kid" was one of the phrases that made its way back to my mom from one of our more distant relatives, but she was unmoved. "They are who they are," she said of her kids, and told everyone I was fine and to leave me alone. Sure enough, twenty or thirty minutes after a meltdown, I'd come out of my room and climb into her lap.

Both of my parents accepted all of us kids just as we were. I don't mean they were lax about discipline. My mom hates bad language, for example, and (poor thing, she's horrified by this now) would occasionally wash out our mouths with soap if we cursed. But in all the ways that matter, she and my dad were liberal, supportive parents, with no fixed ideas about how we should act or who we should be.

My mom wasn't fazed when Rachael was too shy to speak up in kindergarten, didn't freak out when I screamed and ran to my room, and after spending a few days in my first-grade classroom with Mrs. Walmart, she decided nothing was really amiss. Above all, she was calm when, at the age of five, I announced that I wanted to cut my hair short like Brian's and wear only boys' clothes from then on. I loved my twin, but my brother, who was five years older than us, was everything I wanted to be: funny, clever, cheerful, popular, outgoing, and good at all sports.

My mom took it completely in stride. While Rachael kept her hair long and went on wearing skirts, I ran along beside her like her boy twin, while strangers addressed me as "Hey, buddy! Hey, little guy!" I found this hilarious. "Hi!" I would respond beaming, without correcting them. My mom, meanwhile, who is the precise opposite of those mothers who put headbands on bald babies in case strangers think their little girl is a boy, merely said, "I love that she's a tomboy, doesn't she look cute?" One day in first grade, I came in from the playground, stood in the doorway of the classroom with my hands on my hips, and bellowed in Mrs. Walmart's general direction, "Brian Rapinoe is my brother, and I'm just like him!" No wonder she couldn't stand me.

2

STRONG WOMEN

W e're an athletic family, and all of us are athletically built. My dad is compact, stocky. My mom is slender and strong. (She likes to joke that I have her legs, and at some point could she please have them back?) But even compared to the rest of our family, Rachael and I were physically gifted. We figured out how to crawl out of our cribs really young. At age four, after only a few attempts, we rode our bikes without training wheels. When Brian did a trick with a soccer ball, all we needed was to watch him once to have it down pat. Our older siblings regarded us as freaks. As a child, says my sister Jenny, she remembers looking at us running around the yard and thinking, "My sisters are going to get gold medals one day."

At that age, all Rachael and I wanted to do

was have fun, and given our family's interests, it's not surprising that sports were a big outlet. There was a huge oak tree in our yard, and from the time we could first walk, we would chase soccer balls around and around it. We spent hours playing one-on-one basketball in the yard, and "doing drills"—running back and forth between cones—set up by Brian on the lawn. When we weren't playing sports we were watching them. Football, baseball, basketball, hockey, it didn't matter what, we were fans. My dad, who spent his early childhood in Chicago, was a big Cubs fan, and Rachael and I quickly got into the Bulls. Basketball was our first love, and long before we put up posters of the 1999 World Cup champion US Women's National Team, the walls of our bedroom were covered in life-size posters of Michael Jordan.

Of all the sports, soccer was probably the one with which my parents were least familiar. My brother Michael had been into baseball and snowboarding, Jenny was a dancer and cheerleader, and CeCé was into volleyball. Only Brian took up soccer, and by the time we were five and he was ten, he was playing with a local team called the Mavericks. Rachael and I tagged along to his practices and watched the boys like hawks. Every time they did something cool, we ran up and down the sidelines trying to imitate them, until eventually our antics were noticed.

When we were six, we were invited to play with the Under-8 boys' team, since there wasn't a girls' team available. We jumped at the chance.

From the beginning, I just loved it. We were so hyped to play. I loved basketball, track, and, eventually—although it took a while—swimming, but there was something about the ritual of soccer that was special. Every Saturday morning before practice, I got up super early to put on my uniform, so that by the time my mom and sister were ready, I'd be by the door, cleats on, shin guards in, impatient to get in the car. I loved the clicking sound my cleats made on the floor and I loved my team uniform. We played in white T-shirts with black piping at the collar, which through overwear soon faded to brown. Rachael and I were finicky about our gear, and you could hear us hollering down the street: "Mom, fix our shirts!"

In my entire history of playing, I have probably never dominated a team like I did that team of small boys in the early 1990s. Rachael and I were unbeatable. When we got older and hit our teens, the playing pool got bigger and the kids got better. But at ages six, seven, eight, nine, we performed at a level so far and away above everyone else that Fritz, our coach, could only stand on the sidelines and remark to my parents, "They're going to be in the World Cup one day."

A large part of this was natural ability. We

moved fluidly, with instinctive hand-eye coordination and physical fearlessness. But our ferocity also had a lot to do with the fact that we played against each other all the time. This is where having a twin comes in handy. Rachael and I learned a lot by playing against Brian and our older cousins, but our toughest competitors were each other. Every day after school, we played in our yard or across the street at Cow Creek Community Church, which had a soccer field out back. After riding our bikes over there, we'd dump them on the grass and play for as long as the light held, neither of us giving an inch, perfectly matched in ability and drive.

The sheer pitch of our ambition was probably stoked by twin rivalry, which in our case didn't mean wanting to outdo each other, but wanting for the other what we wanted for ourselves: to perform up to our absolute limits. This was evident especially on the field during games. When one of us messed up or gave less than 100 percent, the other would swoop down on her and scream insults while the rest of the team looked on in horror. (I think the rage dump came, in part, from the fact that we knew each other so well; each of us could instantly spot when the other was underperforming. But it's also true that we simply couldn't hear how we sounded. To us, yelling at top volume at each other was completely normal.) It's a big advantage when you're trying to get better at something to spend all your time with someone who can be completely honest with you without fear of losing your love.

We knew we were good. But as a sport, soccer is a relatively slow burn and the team structure means you don't shine all the time. There are no child prodigies in soccer the way there are in, say, gymnastics. In fact, after those first few years in our tiny team in Palo Cedro, we lost a lot. When we were ten, we were invited to try out for the Mavericks' competitive Under-12 boys' team, and we played with them for one season and basically got shellacked every game. After that, my dad decided to set up a girls' team. He and my mom scouted preteen athletes from Red Bluff all the way out to Mount Shasta, getting together a group of fourteen or fifteen girls who my dad coached and managed. We did that for a few years before being scouted by Elk Grove, a much bigger competitive girls' team based down in Sacramento. At that point things started to take off.

All of this happened organically. We loved soccer, and our parents encouraged us, but they did so with no particular end goal in mind. They loved sports, but I think if we'd been into acting, or singing, or violin, or chess, they would still have done everything they could to enable us. It's interesting to consider the difference between the gifted child athlete who goes on to play at the highest level and the one who drops out or remains a recreational player. Obviously the involvement of the parents is a big issue, but probably less so than the temperament of the child. If our parents had ever had to nag us to practice, or drag us out of bed at 4:00 a.m. for the two-hour drive south to Sacramento, we wouldn't have gone the distance. As it was, from age six onward, Rachael and I were completely obsessed, entirely dedicated, and, bizarrely for that age, fanatically self-motivated about playing.

I don't know where this compulsion came from. There were no professional sportswomen in my background. There were, however, a lot of badass women doing things that were considered slightly controversial for their time. One of these was Anna, my maternal great-grandmother—my mom's mom's mom—whose name I have as my middle name. Her family came to the US from Germany at the turn of the twentieth century, settling with a lot of other German immigrants in Rhineland, Texas, where they became farmers. After Anna married Aloysius, my mom's grandfather, in the early 1930s, she gave birth to seven kids, raised her own chickens and pigs, and helped manage the farm. Ten years into the marriage, her husband died of tuberculosis, leaving Anna to run the entire 640 acres alone.

It's a very American story. Anna was really smart, my mom said, and unusually for that time, her husband had insisted she go out on the farm with him and learn the business. She learned how to buy and sell cattle, raise wheat and cotton, and handle herself as the only woman among men. She was very tough, very kind, and very capable. When my mom was a child, Anna would travel from Texas to visit them in San Bernardino, and the house—chaotic with my mom's seven siblings and her alcoholic dad—would brighten up while she was there. Bread would be baked; surfaces would be cleaned. Even my mom's dad would cheer up momentarily. Her motto, said my mom, was "Let's get this done."

When Rachael and I were eighteen months old, our mom realized that the only way for her to work and still see her kids was to work at night—her own mom had done the same thing—and after asking around, she applied for a job at Jack's Grill. Word on the street was that it was such a great place to work that no one ever left, and sure enough, thirty-two years later, my mom still works four shifts a week there.

I love Jack's. It's my second home. My mom's fellow waitresses and their kids, all of whom I've known my whole life, are my second family. When I go back to Redding these days, I'm as excited to visit Jack's as anywhere in town. The restaurant is a legend in the area, established in

1938 and consisting of one cozily lit room with an old-fashioned bar, a tin ceiling, and the best New York strip steak in the world. If it were in an East Coast city, there'd be a line round the block, and as kids, we thought it was the most glamorous place in the world. After school, Rach and I would go sit on the bar stools, eat crackers, and feel the thrill of being part of the scene.

Because my mom didn't get back from her shift until after 11:00 p.m., our only chance to talk to her about stuff was first thing in the morning. Every day before school, she'd be in the kitchen or her chair in the living room, glasses on, hair wild, in her jammies, jacking up on coffee and talking to us. We'd give her a kiss and a hug, sit on her lap, and tell her what we had going on. We'd ask what she was making to put in the fridge for my dad to heat up for dinner. This routine went on all our lives, and even in high school we'd still sit on her lap. My mom remembers being at a soccer tournament in Baltimore, hanging out in a hotel lobby with Rach and I, gangly teenagers, one on each knee, while the other mothers looked on in amazement. But to us it was natural. Mammers is a gem.

It was during one of those morning sessions that we told our mom about the bully in fifth grade. She wasn't picking on us, but she was targeting a weaker kid and we both hated it. My sister and I have this in common: nothing riles us up more than bullying, cheating, or unfairness. It's an almost physical sensation of not being able to stand it or to shut up about it after the event. We told our mom about the girl and about how, after we'd stepped in, her eighth-grade sister had threatened to bring her friends to the playground for a fight. Rachael was more assertive than I was at that age, but I was right behind her. You don't get to do this, we told the kid. Bring it.

Obviously these instincts came from somewhere. Both my parents insisted that you don't let people intimidate you and that you take care of your siblings and family. There was a flip side to this lesson, however: No one is better than you, they said, but equally, you shouldn't think that because you're good at sports, popular, and cute, you're better than anyone else. They taught Rachael and me to recognize how lucky we were—pointed out that things came easily for us, not just in sports, but socially, too—and told us not to take it for granted. Look and see what other people have, they said, because they have something special, too.

To my mom, these lessons were rooted in the Church, although by the time Rachael and I were born, she had walked away from the Catholics— mainly because they'd given her such a hard time for divorcing her first husband, Bill. All us kids were baptized Catholics, but growing up we were taken to a nondenominational church, and while my mom wanted to expose us to faith, she also felt it was our journey, our choice. And anyway, it wasn't about religion. It was about empathy. My mom told the story of being a teenager in Southern California, and how after her dad had been yelling at the kids one day, she turned to her grandmother, Anna, and said, "I can't stand him. I wish he'd just leave." Anna's reply always stayed with my mom: "Oh, Neesy, he's sick, honey. He's just sick." Her dad had been a tyrant, but even so, some compassion was called for.

Still, nothing spins my wheels like an unfair fight, and the same goes for Rachael. We're not looking for an altercation, but we're not going to back down from what's right. It's always been part of our spirit, so much so that there's no decision to make. When we told our mom a pack of eighth-grade girls was coming to fight us, she was alarmed and wanted to go talk to the principal. But we persuaded her not to. We've got this, we said. It seemed important to work it out for ourselves, and after standing our ground, the big kids left, as bullies tend to when they're confronted. That wasn't even the most important thing that happened that day, which was that our friends came to our aid. The best way to beat bullies is to fight them together.

3

PRACTICE

The term "soccer mom" has become a kind of joke, a sexist label for suburban moms that implies a life of indolence and ease. The truth is that being a soccer mom or dad, at least one with a kid who travels for games, is a massive commitment and a ton of hard work. It's exhausting, expensive, and time-consuming, and it means you miss out on a lot of other things. For six years, from the age of eleven through seventeen, every weekend morning began at 4:00 a.m. for my family, when my parents, my sister, and I would pile into the minivan for the long drive to Sacramento, for practice or an 8:00 a.m. game.

A word about minivans: ugh. My family was so big we always had to have one, and as kids we didn't consider them cool. (As adults, it's the one car none of us will drive; my sister Jenny stretched to an Expedition once, but that's as far as she'd go.) Back then, however, they were the only practical choice, and those weekend journeys were wild. My mom, who'd had about four hours sleep after getting in from the restaurant the night before, would roll into the van with her coffee and doze all the way there. My dad, equally exhausted after a hard week, would take the wheel while my sister and I sat in the back. We didn't have time or money for vacations, so those journeys—not just to Sacramento, but as we got older, all over the state, and eventually the country—turned into mini road trips. My mom would look up awesome places to eat on the road, directing us off the highway in search of an out-of-the-way restaurant, until my dad—ravenous, less committed to the search for the perfect chicken parm than the rest of us—would explode, "Can we PLEASE. JUST. STOP. HERE," and be shouted down from the back of the van.

In soccer, finding your own style on the field is as much about self-discovery as it is about practicing and strengthening your skills. As a young kid, you chase after the ball along with everyone else, kicking it more or less haphazardly toward the goal. It's only as you get older and more proficient that, while understanding you have to work as a team, you start to develop your own personality and flair. The girls' soccer league in

Sacramento was tougher than anything we were used to in Redding, and it was obvious to me even then that I was never going to be the strongest or fastest player on the field. To succeed, I would need to develop a style rooted in something other than beating people through physical force.

In 1996, the year we started traveling for games and playing competitively for the Mavericks, I had no idea what that style might turn out to be. At eleven, I was still very much a little kid. I ran around making fart noises. I was a goofball, always doing impressions. (My one of Jim Carrey in **Ace Ventura: Pet Detective** brought the house down for years.) I loved making my family laugh, especially CeCé, who I'd wait for in the kitchen, and when she walked in, I'd stick out my butt and do a funny voice like it was talking. (You had to be there, I guess.) Being a mimic means interspersing periods of performance with periods of watchfulness, and even as a child I'd enjoyed standing off to one side, observing people and situations that interested me. My mom tells the story of how she'd watched me at one of Brian's soccer games once, when I was around five. I have no memory of it, but she recalls how, after spending ten minutes or so studying a teenager on the sidelines whose pose—elbow on knee, one knee over the other—I was clearly fascinated by, I crept up behind him and got myself into the exact same position.

Imitating people like this came naturally to me and was just something I did for fun. It wasn't defensive; I'd never felt the need to camouflage myself by copying others. Of the two of us, I was still more assertive than Rachael, and every day at recess I hit the playground hard, still wearing "boys' clothes," as I'd been doing since kindergarten. The one time my mom managed to get me out of shorts and sneakers was when I was ten years old and we'd gone to a wedding in Texas, and even then she'd had to trick me. My mom's aunt's son was getting married at a fancy country club, and when I told my mom there was no way I was wearing a dress, she'd sneakily said, "OK, well, we're staying at a great hotel in Dallas where you can swim and play games, but you'll probably be happier staying at home." I ended up in a moderately acceptable sundress, alongside Rachael in a big frilly pink one.

That year we turned eleven, the one significant change was that Rachael had a growth spurt and now was taller than me—five foot four to my four foot eleven, at the end of fifth grade. If it was a sign of things to come, it seemed, along with everything else going on, like no big deal at the time. My sister Jenny moved out, but still lived in Redding. CeCé went away to college, but came home all the time. (On her arrival, Rach and I would always run down the driveway yelling,

"Cissy! Cissy!" before throwing ourselves into her arms.) The trouble with Brian hadn't really registered yet, and even by my family's standards, it was a quiet period. And then I turned up for the first day of sixth grade.

It was as if everyone got a memo over the summer and I missed it. It was quick, and it was jarring, and I had no idea what was going on. All of a sudden, the girls didn't run around with the boys anymore. Gender roles became sharply defined. Sitting around and chatting was a girl thing; charging around after a ball was for boys. Wearing shorts and sneakers became, if not a cause for social rejection exactly, still definitely not something other girls were doing. And while being good at sports had always guaranteed me a certain confidence and popularity that carried over into the classroom, that dynamic was no longer assured. I wasn't picked on or bullied, but I didn't know where I fit in or how to behave. I felt suddenly, deeply uncomfortable.

The craziest thing about all this is that somehow my twin did get the memo. Having been the quieter of the two of us for most of our lives, overnight Rachael turned into a social butterfly. She dressed right and boys liked her. She made plans and hung out with people. My mom tried to help by suggesting I could be sporty and tomboyish and still find a cool dress to wear, but I didn't know where to start. Thank god for Rachael. For the whole of sixth grade and a few years after that, she basically managed the style and social decisions for both of us. I bought what she told me to buy (anything popular) and tried to ride on her coattails socially. "Rach, what are we going to wear?" I would say each morning, and for the rest of the day would try to stay as near to her as possible. There were times when I walked so closely behind Rachael I was literally running on her heels.

If someone had told me I was gay back then, I might've been like, "**Oh**, OK, got it." (Actually, I probably would've instinctively pushed back against the label and snapped, "No, I'm not.") All things being equal, however—if everyone knew their sexuality right away without it being an issue—I don't think I would've felt uncomfortable about it. The problem was I didn't know **what** was going on and the uncertainty bothered me. People in my family are self-possessed and have definite style—not my dad, obviously, who goes around in clothes fourteen sizes too big for him—but my mom and my siblings are all very confident, and one of the ways they express themselves is through clothes. When my mom puts on a crisp white shirt every night to go work at Jack's, she's like an actress preparing for the stage. There's a version of her life in which, having looked after first her siblings, then us, she might have turned into a domestic martyr, but that's not my mom, who practiced self-care before there was even a word for it. She has always been like: I'm getting dressed, I'm going to get my jewelry and do my hair, because looking good is a way to be independent. I wanted to be like that—decisive, self-confident, never overwhelmed by the circumstances around me. Instead, I was just awkward.

I told myself not to panic. I was a late bloomer, I thought. That's all it was: I was simply late to the party, and if I didn't want to be super feminine or have crushes on boys yet, it went hand in hand with the fact that I didn't get any taller until the end of sixth grade, or get my period until I was almost fourteen. It wasn't even that I didn't find boys attractive. It was more that I would look at a boy and have this feeling of **I don't know if he's cute or not.** I just don't know! It's not moving the needle, so I've got no idea! But I didn't feel nonsexual or have crushes on girls, either. Those years were completely mystifying.

If this sounds like denial or repression, it didn't seem that way at the time. Redding wasn't exactly liberal in those days, and even now there are churches not far from my parents' house that practice "conversion therapy"—praying over gays to straighten them out. Within our family, however, there was no homophobic talk. I knew my mom had been Catholic, but I didn't consider the Catholic Church's position on gays, or anything else for that matter, as having anything to do with me. And at school, while the word "gay" in the 1990s was slang for "bad," when people said, "Oh, that's so gay," in the normal flow of things, it didn't seem to me, at the time, like anyone meant anything by it.

My older sister, Jenny, is bi, and she had a serious girlfriend when I was growing up. No one ever spoke explicitly about her sexual orientation or who she was dating—it would simply be "Oh, this is Jenny's friend," rather than "This is her girlfriend, and Jenny's gay, this is a big gay relationship"—but without officially knowing it, I still knew, plus she always had gay friends. To this day I'll say to her, "Fuck you, you should've told me I was gay, what were you thinking?" Although I know what she was thinking, which was: "I'm not going to be the one to bring it up. Mom's going to be pissed to have another one on her hands." (As it turned out, one more gay in the family was a low estimate.)

This makes my mom sound homophobic, which she wasn't. She just wanted her children to have an easy path through life, and to her generation gay meant hard, or at least harder. Anyway, as

far as I was concerned, I wasn't gay. In my freshman year of high school, a boy named Josh asked
me out, and although I couldn't tell if he was cute
or not, it seemed like a good idea to say yes. We
got along great. I liked him a lot. We dated for
months and never **did anything.** It's so funny,
looking back: we never took a single step forward
sexually. More months went by and still nothing
happened. I think I wanted to do more—or at
least I didn't **not** want to do more—but he didn't
really push, so things never advanced. Then we
broke up. That was Josh. It's totally hilarious to
me now.

One result of all this confusion was that I
drilled down further into my life in sports. I had
a built-in community there, not just in soccer
but in the other activities Rachael and I excelled
at—basketball and track—and my success on
the field was just enough to keep my confidence
afloat. We were still playing competitively with
the Mavericks, touring every weekend in the
Sacramento Youth Soccer League, and then
the summer I turned fourteen, when we joined
Elk Grove, a much bigger team, soccer was suddenly big news. In 1999, the FIFA Women's World
Cup was staged in the US, and after reaching the
final, the US won 5–4 against China, in front of
a crowd of ninety thousand people at the Rose
Bowl—still a record crowd for a women's game
in the US.

I remember watching those games on TV and being thrilled. I knew the World Cup would be big, but whoa; I had no idea women's soccer could pull such a crowd. Still, I didn't watch the final and think, That could be me. As a dream, it seemed impossibly far off; clearly I was too small and didn't run fast enough to have a hope in hell of getting to that level. It wasn't just that. Rachael and I loved to play, but we weren't exactly planning our careers yet. I sympathize with modern parents, who are sold this idea that if you do the right things—have your child join this club, do that camp, meet this coach—you can pretty much map out their route to sports stardom. It's a misconception. Of all the kids who start out in soccer, 99.9 percent will never play professionally. The only true path is to free your child to have fun and see what happens.

If Rachael and I didn't hunger to play in the pros, we did put up a poster of the US Women's National Team on our wall and enjoy the fact that players like Mia Hamm and Brandi Chastain were suddenly household names. Everything else in life felt so complicated and, in our family at least, was becoming one hundred times more so thanks to my brother, but here the rules were straightforward: you won or you lost, you were good or bad. It was that simple. Years later, when I played in the World Cup final in front of a TV audience of 82 million people, I would find the narrowness of most professional athletes—their tendency to behave as if nothing outside of winning matters—not only limiting, but wrong. But for a brief period of adolescence, that childish tunnel vision was a heavenly refuge.

4

BRIAN

The way my family tells it, as a young kid, I idolized my brother Brian. And I guess, what with the hair, and the clothes, and the being into soccer—and the "Brian Rapinoe's my brother, and I'm just like him!"—it must be true. In all honesty, though, I can't really remember. I look at pictures of my brother from when we were kids and I have a certain fond feeling. He had all kinds of naughty magazines, I remember **that**. But I don't have many definitive early memories of him, positive or negative. This might sound overdramatic, but the later memories of Brian have come to be so dominant, they block almost everything else out.

This is the truth about having a drug user in the family: it never ends. You get on with your life, and everything carries on as normal, but the feeling of devastation never goes away. I was on a plane to Europe recently, watching a movie starring Julia Roberts about a drug addict kid who comes home for Christmas, and suddenly I was crying. It hit too close to home. It felt exactly like the story of my family growing up, and that story is so raw, emotionally, still. My parents were always honest about Brian and he was never a source of shame, either at home or at school. We learned to talk about his problems, to say, Yeah, my brother is fucking wild, and to absorb what happened to him as healthily as we could. That doesn't mean our hearts aren't broken. What are you going to do? It's incredibly sad and incredibly hard, and whatever happens, it will always be that way.

It was a generational thing, or it was bad luck, or bad timing, but whatever it was, Brian got into it. In the last twenty years, opioids have killed more than 450,000 people in the US, a large number of them in and around Redding. My hometown has the classic profile of a rural area hit hard by the opioid crisis, a hollowed-out former industrial center where lots of people, many of them suffering pain from manual work, were overprescribed opioids. In recent years, Redding has recorded one of the highest rates of opioid pills per capita of almost anywhere in the country, while the overdose rate is more than triple the statewide average.

All of this was just beginning in the mid-1990s, when I was ten and Brian was fifteen. Maybe he started taking drugs earlier than that, smoking weed or whatever, but the first real memory I have regarding his drug use is of our parents sitting us down after dinner one night to tell us that Brian was about to be in the local newspaper. Rachael and I were in the paper all the time because of soccer, but this was different: Brian had been arrested at school for possession of meth. Even though it was a first offense, he'd had so much on him that the case went to court and he was sent to juvenile detention. Everything unraveled from there.

Or rather, things went back to normal, then collapsed, then renormalized before collapsing again, and so it went on, around and around. As anyone who has lived with an addict knows, the descent happens in fits and starts, and for long periods it can seem as if things are OK. Brian would be back at school, attending drug rehab, seemingly getting himself back on track. Then slowly the signs would start to resurface.

My sister and I didn't understand much of it, at first. We were too young, and anyway, we were preoccupied with our own lives. I was going through my period of social awkwardness, Rachael was busy being popular, and every weekend we were crushing it at soccer. It didn't seem abnormal to us if our brother disappeared for long periods, either into his room or outside the house, and reemerged looking strung out on the sofa.

And there were stretches when Brian would seem to be fine. It's one of the misconceptions about drug abuse that it only strikes those who are unhappy, or misfits, or from terrible homes—all dumb clichés, none of them true. You can't tell by looking at someone, or their family, if they're likely to use drugs, and when Brian was clean, he was amazing. Everyone loved him. He was calm, and chill, and funny, and charming, and right up through high school, there was cachet to being his sister. In his early teens, he had been as into soccer as we were, traveling on the weekends for games with the Mavericks, going to practice and hanging out with us at halftime. This is when he'd have us do drills around the cones, then let us take shots at the goal as a reward. He loved that he could teach the game to us, and we loved learning from him—or at least this is the image my mom has painted for me, along with the one of us hunkered down in front of the TV, three loving siblings together. It's painful to think about now. When Brian got into drugs, we didn't just lose him, we lost the memories of who he had been.

As we got older, we learned to recognize the

signs. My mom's brother had had drug and alcohol problems. I had a friend whose dad was a heroin addict and who'd been sober for a long time and ran a recovery center in Redding; Brian would end up going there for a while. And one of our neighbors' kids died of an overdose from a fentanyl patch. But until Brian started using, we really had no idea what it was like. There's a period when you know but you don't know, when you're still putting little details together and figuring it out. Brian hogging the bathroom was always a big sign. He'd be in there for what seemed like hours in the morning while my sister and I, teenage girls obsessed with how we looked, banged on the door, yelling at him to get out of the shower so we could get ready for school. There'd be another red flag when we walked into the kitchen and opened a draw to find no fucking spoons; Brian had taken them all. Eventually, the signs were so stark you couldn't mistake them: holy shit, a syringe in his room, and all this drug paraphernalia in the bathroom. Finally we understood he was using in the house.

In the late 1990s and early 2000s, meth abuse was rampant around Redding, but thank god that, early on, Brian ditched meth for pills and heroin. It's probably why he's still alive; you can't do meth for a long time and survive. With heroin, once you're a long-term user, you're just doing it to maintain your baseline and it doesn't always come with a lot of chaotic energy. Even when he was using, Brian was calm and chill, either asleep or downing and totally out of it. If he was on a crazy bender, he simply wouldn't be home.

My parents knew he was using in the house. I think they thought it was better for him to be doing it there, where he was safe, and where they could do everything possible to try to get him to stop. And they did try everything. They sent him to military school in Mississippi. They enrolled him in every kind of drug rehabilitation program. I think my dad found him a job in construction, so he was working, off and on, while still taking heroin. Things would calm down for a while and we'd let ourselves hope, then we'd get home from school one day and our parents would be crying. We became wearyingly accustomed to what came next—the announcement that "Brian's been arrested again."

There is another truth about drug addicts, and by extension those who serve time in prison: While, as human beings, they are valued by society at nothing, their symbolic value to the system is huge. For "us" to be "good," "they" must be "bad"—and not just bad, but irredeemably so. It's classic divide and rule, them and us, and it makes rehabilitation almost impossible. It also ensures that those entering the system are put beyond the reach of our common humanity. The way people serving time are spoken of reminds me of the myth peddled by right-wing politicians—that the only difference between the rich and the poor is the latter's own fecklessness. If you are a "repeat offender," it's not because of structural failings within the system, just as if you are a drug addict, it's not because opioid manufacturers aggressively marketed their drugs at you until you were hooked. Instead, you are in jail, or an addict, because that is, at root, who you are. This is the nightmare Brian, my kind, funny, lovely brother, got into as a teenager and is still in today. He was not the "bad" child who went off the rails, just as Rachael and I weren't the "good" kids who didn't put a foot wrong. I don't absolve my brother entirely of blame, but it was always much bigger and more complicated than him.

It started when I was thirteen and Brian was eighteen, when he was sent to prison for stealing a car. This was the first time he'd been sentenced as an adult, and the beginning of his life inside. Over the next twenty years, he would be in and out of jail—including stints in Pelican Bay and Susanville, notoriously violent federal prisons in Northern California—for a total of sixteen years, half of them spent in solitary confinement. Outside prison, Brian was just a druggie, stealing to buy heroin, but basically a docile and amenable person. On the inside, he was a violent gang member, frequently having his sentence extended for possession of drugs and deadly weapons, and for assault.

It was impossible to reconcile the brother we had known with this new image of Brian, or to understand how, while Rachael and I were heading into ninth grade and starting to attract the interest of bigger soccer teams, Brian was in prison joining a white supremacist gang. The way he explained it to our mom afterward was that inside, the races are segregated and organized into gangs, and if you're going to survive—particularly if you get into trouble, as Brian did—then you'd better affiliate quickly. He never talked to us about it, and he never tried to "convert" us to white supremacy. As far as I know, when he was out, he never went to white power rallies or did anything remotely connected to his life inside (apart from take drugs). It was exclusively a prison persona, adopted as a survival measure to give him a sense of power and identity. None of which made it any easier when, at nineteen, he came home from that first stint in jail with a homemade swastika tattoo on one hand.

Like millions of prisoners whose main crime is addiction, Brian shouldn't have been inside in the first place. Why do we even have private prisons, the primary purpose of which is to make money, not to care for or rehabilitate the prisoners? Brian had a drug problem and committed crimes and was out of control and all that, but if you send a drug addict to prison, he's not going to get sober, which means he's more likely to reoffend. Then he comes out, has a group of friends who have all been inside, too, can't vote, has no resources, and has to try to get a job with a felony on his record. If regular people can't get jobs—which in Redding they couldn't—the applicant who just got out of prison sure as hell isn't going to. It's such a mess.

We didn't talk about Brian's problems as part of a larger picture. We didn't need to; we understood without having to articulate it. I didn't learn about the broken prison system, or racism in the criminal justice system, or how the races are pitted against one another by people in power in a political theory class or by reading about it in the newspaper—although much later, in my twenties, I would go out of my way to educate myself. But at a critical point in my adolescence, it was in my home, day in, day out: the reality of how a broken system fails the most vulnerable, and how once you're in it, it can be almost impossible to get out.

We weren't always sympathetic. My brother continued to be in and out of prison and to go through cycles of sobriety and relapse, and while, as young kids, Rachael and I had felt scared and sorry for him, as we got older, we got mad at all the pain he was causing. I went to visit him a couple of times when he was in Shasta County Jail, but I wouldn't travel farther; and once he was in Susanville and Pelican Bay, both miles away from anywhere and involving a whole complex process of visitation, that was it; I was done. My parents didn't visit him much, either. They told him, We'll always love you, talk to you, and send you money, but beyond a certain point we're done with your fucking antics, besides which, hello, we're actually busy raising your child. Austin was born when Brian was twenty-one and we were sophomores in high school, to a mom who, like our brother, had a history of drug abuse. My parents stepped in immediately. Austin, who is nineteen now and a firefighter, has never known any other parental figures.

The irony is that because of Brian, Rachael and I were probably much better behaved than we might otherwise have been. Anytime we were tempted to rebel, we'd both think, Jesus Christ, Brian was a drug addict at fifteen and then in jail. OK, we're not going to do that. We weren't big drinkers in our teens and we didn't stay out late, partly because we always had practice the next day and partly because we'd seen our parents go through enough with our brother. Rachael once hid in the trunk of a car to sneak out of school in the middle of the day and was put in detention

("Good," said our mom), and as far as I can re-call, that was it.

And we were busy. A year after our brother came out of prison, Rachael and I went to Foot-hill High School, where Brian had gone and was still fondly remembered. We did drama and were on the student council. We played lots of sports besides soccer. We were lucky—we had found something we were good at and loved at a very early age, and it basically carried us through ado-lescence. But we also understood that to go for-ward we would have to be good at other things, too. I wasn't top of the class, but I was always on the honor roll and mindful about keeping up my academic average; I wasn't going to get Cs and Ds and blow my chances of what seemed, at the time, like the furthest my soccer career might take me: a scholarship to college.

This heady prospect became a lot more real when, at fourteen, Rachael and I were scouted by the Olympic Development Program, a national youth training organization that exposed us to better coaches and players. Soon after that, we began playing for Elk Grove and ferrying back and forth to Sacramento. Elk Grove wasn't the biggest or best team. In fact, a few years later, when we started playing in college scouting tour-naments, we were often the underdogs and our coach was as excited by the talent scouts as we

were. ("They're all lined up!" he'd say breath-
lessly, looking at the guys with clipboards standing under the floodlights on the sidelines.)
Slowly, however, we started making our way up
the national rankings. In 2003, we came second
in the Girls' Under-18 US Youth Soccer National
Championships, losing to the Peachtree City
Lazers in the final game, in which I scored the
equalizing goal. And we watched as players a little older than us won full soccer scholarships.

One day when I was sixteen, the phone rang.
It was a representative from the US Under-17
Women's National Team, inviting me to play for
an international youth game in France. A few
weeks later, a huge parcel arrived in the mail,
addressed to me and overflowing with USA-
branded loot: shin pads, sweatshirts, T-shirts,
polo shirts, cleats, the whole nine yards. A few
weeks after that, I was in France, pulling on the
USA shirt for the first time, a series of events
so implausible I could hardly process them: the
call-up, the free stuff, the application for my first
passport, followed by the plane ride to France
and the game—I'd never experienced anything
like it.

Still, I didn't think it would lead to anything.
Being picked for the youth side was a huge deal,
but it didn't guarantee or even raise much of a
hope of anything more. The national youth sides
drew from a huge pool of young players, most

of whom would never play nationally again, and I didn't know anyone who'd made a career out of soccer. The furthest Rachael and I could see was still college. We might wildly dream of one day playing in the Olympics, but it was hard to square with the reality of our mostly smallish league games in California.

And we still lost a lot, something I didn't always handle that well. My brother Michael came to watch us play in a tournament in San Diego one time. Like the rest of us, he's super competitive with an amped-up personality. He's also big into sports. After fighting really hard, we lost the game, and when we came off the field, we were bummed. So was my brother. As Rachael and I sat on the ground drinking water and commiserating with the coach, Michael started mouthing off. "I can't believe you lost!" he said. "You had that game! I can't believe it!"

My mom considers me the most chill of all her kids, and it's true that since my early temper tantrums had died down, I was generally pretty relaxed. But when I lose it, I lose it, and I was already mad with myself for blowing the game. I looked up at my brother. A week earlier, he'd had a front tooth knocked out in a fight and it hadn't been fixed yet. "You think you could do better, you toothless, inbred, backwoods degenerate?" I said. I didn't yell, but I was vicious, and everyone stopped talking and stared. I didn't mean to be

cruel, but when I'm attacked, I can sometimes re-
taliate too hard. Though on that occasion, I still
think he deserved it.

We missed out on a lot because of our playing schedule. There were no weekend sleepovers,
hardly any parties, and I think I went to one prom
and one formal dance throughout high school.
We did have limits, though. The conventional
path for a player with talent at that age is to graduate to playing for your state team. Rachael and I
both made the cut. But after going to a couple of
regional training camps and touring the country
with the California team for a few months, we
decided it involved too much travel and quit. We
actually had a life at high school. Of the two of
us, Rachael was still the more socially dynamic—
after school, I would generally be on the couch,
watching sports, and yelling to her, "What are
we doing later?" while she ran around making
plans—but things had settled down since middle
school and I had good friends. We weren't alphas,
but we had earned respect, particularly when I
helped win competitions for our entire grade.
Rachael and I didn't play soccer for our high
school team, which was too small for us by then,
but in our junior year we played in the school's
annual powder puff football game, a hugely
competitive tradition in which the junior girls
played the seniors, and every year the seniors

won—except the year Rachael and I played, when the juniors won 65–10.

Still, in spite of our OK social lives and all the hours on the field, the people we spent the most time with in our teens were our parents. It's an overlooked aspect of being a soccer mom or dad that you will probably hang out with your adolescents more than you did when they were toddlers. At an age when most of our friends were off partying, we were with our parents in the minivan. After all the drama with Brian, it felt healing to hang with them, and we were also stupendously grateful. It's not a characteristic generally associated with teenagers, but we would have to have been stupid not to appreciate what they did for us—not just the getting up so early every Saturday, but all the money they spent on travel as well as tournament and coaching fees, when their finances were already strained.

They still watched us like hawks. My mom is prone to worrying, and after Brian, she was in a constant spin cycle of terror that one of us would go the same way he did. We would always hear from her about "the dangers of binge drinking," or she'd tell us, "Don't drink and drive," or "If you're walking across a deserted parking lot at night, put your keys in your hand." When we went to college, she would send us endless dire clippings from the newspaper, not just about drugs, but about rape, robbery, and anything else bad that could happen. Rachael had a staph infection in her knee once—just a topical thing—and my mom sent her the story of a girl in college who **lost her leg** after a similar infection. She's such an alarmist that we'd have to tell her, that's crazy, relax, it's not happening to us. But we understood it, too. She and my dad had been so burned by what happened with Brian.

5

OUT

The University of Portland wasn't our first choice; in fact, Rachael and I didn't even want to visit. The city was too cold, too rainy, and the college was too small— only three thousand kids, which we thought was super lame—and too close to Redding, a mere four hundred miles north of home. Our mom put her foot down: before making a decision, we had to see every college that was offering us a scholarship, which is to say every college that saw us play. (The exception was North Carolina, which only gives full scholarships to national team players and had an attitude like, We're the talent and you can come here or not, to which we politely said: not.) We thought we wanted to be near the beach, somewhere like Santa Barbara, or Santa Clara, where the soccer coach was so keen on recruiting us he picked us up from the airport. But after visiting those schools, we had second thoughts; they seemed like party colleges trying too hard to be cool. Rachael and I didn't know what we wanted exactly, but we knew that wasn't us.

At eighteen, we still thought this way—as a single unit. For a second, we had considered applying to different universities, but had just as quickly abandoned the idea. We had such similar tastes we'd probably end up choosing the same college anyway, and why make life harder by depriving ourselves of each other? We couldn't see it at the time, but in fact our lives had already started moving apart. To get to the highest level in soccer, you really have to want it—not just the playing but the lifestyle: the travel, the brutal physical demands, the uncertain career path. In our last year of high school, Rachael was starting to broaden her interests. She still loved to play, but as we looked toward college, she began to be interested in other things, among them medicine and business. Meanwhile, I was still thinking only of soccer.

One weekend in the fall of 2003, we went on a recruitment visit to the University of Portland. It's a private Catholic university with a tuition of forty thousand dollars, and they had offered Rachael and me full scholarships. A year earlier, our friend Stephanie Lopez, a teammate at Elk

Grove, had won a similar scholarship and told us it was amazing, but we weren't entirely convinced. We knew Portland had a good soccer team, but that's all we knew. Looking back, I find this funny. A city so achingly liberal it has become a kind of joke—of course we belonged there. And on that first visit, we both lost our minds. Shrewdly, the university had invited us while it was hosting a big Nike soccer tournament, and on a beautiful fall day when the campus looked stunning. After watching the tournament, we called our mom. "Oh my god, this is it, we love it," we said. The soccer team was cool, the field was amazing, Portland was perfect, and the college vibe jibed with what we were looking for—somewhere that wasn't trying to be anything other than what it was. We were in.

Or at least Rachael was. We accepted the offers in early 2004, and were due to start at Portland the following September. In February, however, I received an astonishing phone call: it was a coach on the US Women's National Team, offering me a spot to play in the FIFA Under-19 Women's World Championship in Thailand later that year. A year earlier, when I'd played for the U-17 team in France, it had felt very much like a one-off. Now a pattern was emerging, and I was so stunned I could hardly relay the information to my parents. Then I looked at the dates. The competition was due to take place over three weeks in November. I would have to defer entry to college until January 2005.

I'm not exactly modest. I knew I was good, and I thought I deserved my place—it's not as if I were running around after the phone call thinking, Oh, it'll just be an honor to be there. And yet winning a spot on the national team came as a huge surprise. I'd never been the best player on my team. And I hadn't taken the conventional path. A lot of the other national team members had come up through their state teams and had been playing for the national side for years, on the Under-14 through Under-18 teams. Compared to them, I was a late developer who had shot out of relative obscurity. And while Rachael and I had been single-minded about soccer, our parents had worked hard to give our lives balance. To be chosen as one of the eleven best players in the country was a very big deal. I couldn't quite believe I was here.

For the first time, Rachael and I would be playing apart, on different sides of the world and for different teams. It was an odd feeling. We had been neck and neck in soccer for so long, and now one of us was pulling ahead. The fact that it was me came as no surprise—Rachael was an incredible athlete, but during the last few years I had become the stronger one. Plus, soccer had already given us everything we wanted: a ticket out of Redding. Years of traveling the country for games had broadened our horizons, and for a while now we'd been desperate to get out.

Still, one of us being chosen while the other wasn't could have harmed our relationship. I think the reason it didn't comes down to how we are with each other. During high school, when Rachael excelled socially, it made my life easier, not harder. We'd always been competitive **for** rather than with each other, seeing ourselves reflected in each other's performance; if one of us was happy, it was half the battle. We were also so frank with each other that rivalry—not the camp drama of teen girls fighting, but real, seething resentment—had no air to breathe. Part of why I have such an honest assessment of myself is that I've always had Rachael in my peripheral vision; it's impossible to hide from the kind of mirror that shouts abuse when you're not up to scratch. When I got the call from the national team, there was no weird jealousy. She was as excited as I was.

The rest of the 2004 season went by in a blur. Every Saturday morning, we got in the van as usual—now with Austin, a toddler, in the back with us—and drove to play with Elk Grove. In June we graduated high school. Rachael and I were psyched to move on, but also grateful for all the support we'd been given and wrote thank-you notes to some of our teachers. I think our parents breathed a sigh of relief, too. We'd gotten through adolescence unscathed, and after all their hard work and sacrifice, things were starting to pay off. When September came, Rachael went to Portland and I started training in earnest with the national team.

It was a good squad, full of future stars. Becky Sauerbrunn, my future national teammate and ally in litigation, was on the team, as were Stephanie Lopez and Amy Rodriguez. And goalkeeper Ashlyn Harris was a prodigy. The Under-19 Women's World Championship wasn't a highly publicized event—if adult women's soccer struggled for attention, the teenagers weren't making any headlines. But it was an amazing experience. There were twelve countries in the tournament, and we played across four venues in three cities—Bangkok, Chiang Mai, and Phuket. I had traveled abroad for a few games before—after that first game in France, to Mexico, and once to China—but this was different: three weeks of games with an average crowd size of eleven thousand, rising in the quarterfinals to a crowd twice that size.

I performed pretty well and scored three goals over the course of the tournament, though I remember more about the spectacle than about the soccer itself. Our highest-scoring game was against Russia in the qualifying round, which we won 4–0, before being knocked out by Brazil in the quarters. (Germany won the tournament, beating China 2–0 in the final.) Our team was given the fair play award, which is a bit like getting a perfect attendance record in school, but it didn't matter. The whole experience was mind-blowing: playing at that level, in front of an international crowd, and while wearing a USA shirt was beyond anything I'd dreamed of. We were in Thailand for a month, and you can imagine, a nineteen-year-old hanging out in Bangkok and on the beach in Phuket—it was wild.

If this was life as a pro soccer player, I was in, and in my excitement, the opportunities looked endless. Just over the horizon were the 2007 FIFA Women's World Cup and the 2008 Olympics. I wasn't one for advance planning, and had no real sense of what a "career" in soccer might look like, but it didn't seem ludicrous to assume this was the beginning of everything.

It's a new world when you go to college. Life is cool and different and you can do whatever you like—stay up late, drink, change your mind about everything. Portland's a small city, but compared to Redding it seemed like a metropolis, and to Rachael and me, the liberal vibe felt like jumping into water after crawling across a desert. I became instantly, massively obnoxious. When I went home, I lectured my parents about conserving energy and recycling (my dad told me wearily he'd been doing both for twenty years). I had voted for George W. Bush in 2004, because that's how everyone else I knew voted, and frankly I'd thought voting at all at that age was highly commendable. But in college, after studying sociology with a minor in political science, I understood for the first time what Democrats and Republicans really were, and that there was no way I was a Republican. Believe me, I let my parents know about the errors in their thinking. The liberal wing of the family, consisting of me, Rach, and our aunt Melanie, started to get under way.

Rachael and I hadn't communicated much during her first semester in Portland, and that continued when I joined her in January. We hung out, but I think we both needed a little time to settle in on our own. I fell in love with the place instantly—the city, the team, the soccer field, which was beautiful, surrounded by trees and with wooded mountains in the distance. And then, a few weeks into my first semester, I looked up during practice one day and realized something extraordinary: I had a crush on one of my teammates.

It wasn't like, oh, suddenly I'm gay. It took a second to figure out what was going on. But while it was happening, it didn't feel negative. It was just . . . normal. For the first time, I was attracted to someone, and the discovery thrilled me. No more limbo, no more weird asexual dates. All those years of missing out, of not feeling what everyone else seemed to be feeling and having no idea why, were over, and any regret I might have experienced about those feelings being for a woman were overwhelmed by a sheer sense of relief. Two things struck me. Number one: Duh, fucking clearly I'm gay and why didn't anyone tell me? And number two: This is awesome.

The speed at which I embraced this new knowledge about myself is, I guess, unusual. It's not as though my parents had a ton—or any—gay friends; and although they weren't homophobes, they weren't super liberal. Growing up, the only out person on TV was Ellen DeGeneres, and we were surrounded by everyday homophobia. If it was normal to trash someone by using "gay" as an epithet—"You're wearing a visor, that's so gay"—that doesn't mean it wasn't homophobic.

And yet I had absolutely no qualms about accepting the fact I was gay. I think some of what I was feeling had to do with Brian. I know plenty of people who, when they come out to their parents, worry they are "letting them down." Brian hadn't let my parents down—he was a person in pain—but given how much time they'd spent worrying about him, I wasn't going to beat myself up for "disappointing" them by being gay. Plus, I didn't honestly think it was going to be a problem. My parents were conventional, but they were never narrow-minded. My mom is a deeply moral person, and she's not judgmental; the same goes for my dad. "Your journey, your choice," she had said when I'd stopped going to church, and she felt that way about everything. My mom is someone who, after a rough start in life, had chosen to be happy, and without even realizing it I had learned from her example. I was so over the moon, so drunk on self-knowledge after so many years of self-doubt, that it was impossible for me to think of being gay as anything but good.

Suddenly, everything fell into place. Since kindergarten, when I'd cut my hair and dressed like my brother, I'd had no decisive instincts about personal style. At nineteen, my look was—oh, dear. With no better ideas, I had defaulted to the classic, upper-middle-class, white soccer-player look, a dishwater blond ponytail, held off my face by—Jesus Christ—a headband. I immediately cut my hair. I abandoned all interest in girls' clothing. I felt free to look like and do precisely what I wanted. A few weeks later, a girl on the college basketball team emailed me over the internal messaging system to say, Hi, wanna go out? My entire life began.

Immediately after my realization, I ran to find Rachael. She and I had drifted apart when it came to religion. I had given it up years earlier, but like our mom, Rachael was still a practicing Christian, which made what happened next much harder for her. When I told her I was gay, she said calmly, "Oh, me too." She'd even dated someone during her first semester, while I was in Thailand. It was almost impossible for us to surprise each other—of course my twin was gay; how could she not have been?—but I was taken aback that she hadn't told me.

I didn't dwell on it for long; I was too busy being delighted with myself. But looking back, Rachael had a much rougher journey than I did. The church she went to was one of those supposedly liberal ones that pretends to be accepting but actually preaches "Hate the sin, love the sinner." Which is, of course, motherfucking-ass homophobic. It's so much worse than regular homophobia, because these people don't think they're homophobic. You're homophobic! And you're hiding behind Christianity! She would be twenty-four before she shook off the last of this thinking and fully embraced her identity as a gay woman.

Our mom was coming to visit and I was going to tell her I was gay. This was not, I was sure, going to be a big deal. "Honestly," I said to Rachael, who remained skeptical of my thinking, "she's going to be totally fine. There is no one gayer than me! She probably already knows."

A few days later, I turned up at my mom's hotel room. After some small talk about the family, I nonchalantly told her, "I'm gay." She looked totally shocked. Then I was totally shocked. "What?!" I said, and burst out laughing. "This is **crazy**! Hello?! How could you not realize this?" When my mom finally found her voice, she said something like "No, you're not," and that's when I flew off the handle. "My whole life makes sense now. I'm fucking ready to roll, and you can either get on board or get the fuck out." Or words to that effect.

If I could go back and do it again, I would probably extend more grace to my mom. On the other hand, I don't think you have to extend grace to people who don't have accepting views. My mom had no moral qualms about homosexuality. It was a protective instinct, premised on the idea that being gay would make my life harder, and if I'd been planning on spending the next forty years in a small, conservative town like Redding, she would probably have been right. Nevertheless, it was annoying, and as we began to talk about it and the conversation got increasingly tense, I created a diversion by looping in Rachael. "Oh, and by the way, she's gay, too," I said. When I left, I called Rach and said, "Hey, I just outed you to Mom." "You really shouldn't have done that," she said.

My mom now says she just needed a minute. (To which Rachael says dryly, "Try six years. Water under the bridge, but—") She needed to process it, she says. "My girls are gay, OK. It's going to take a moment for that to sink in." I don't remember my dad reacting one way or another beyond saying, "OK, whatever, I love you guys," but for my mom it was a bigger deal. She worried it would impact our success, and she worried what her coworkers would say. "I don't want the world to be hard for you, or for people to be negative toward you, or for this to affect you or hurt you in any way." That was how her thinking went, so we finally got to the point where I said, "What exactly is the problem here? Your coworkers have their own lives going on, and if they give it any thought at all, it'll be to think your daughters are in college, playing sports, and doing great, which by the way is completely correct."

I mean, I get it, too. People have hopes and dreams for their kids and it's not even necessarily about being gay; it's about being different from what they had planned. To my mom's credit, she took steps to inform herself. She told me later that she went away and read lots of books about people coming out in their twenties and the feelings they had when they were younger. She also told me she read a bunch of books about homosexuality from a Christian standpoint, "And I didn't agree with any of them."

None of this made it easier for Rachael, whose ambivalence allowed my parents to consider she might just be going through a phase. There was no question of them saying that to me. Rachael and I had switched places again, and for the next few years I was the more confident of the two of us. "The only one who has a fucking problem with this is **you**," I said to my mom that day. "The only one who cares is **you**. The only one saying anything crazy is **you**." We're so similar, my mom and I. We say what we think and then we move on. What I said to her that day is what I say to everyone who thinks it might be better not to be gay: You need to get over it.

6

DOWN

There is no crowd in the world like the college sports crowd. The day before I made my debut for the Portland Pilots, it was as if the whole university was anticipating the game with the same feverish excitement that we were. I heard the drum squad practicing across campus; everywhere you looked, people were in purple and white. The following night, we played Stanford in the opening game of the 2005 season before a crowd the size of the entire student body—3,400 people—who went berserk when we won 3–0. I'm not susceptible to impostor syndrome, but getting in two goals—my first in the opening five minutes, and my second, a header, flicked in at the far post in the thirty-third minute—was a relief. Phew, I had justified my scholarship.

Portland has outstanding records in cross country and baseball, but soccer is the big crowd-pleaser—specifically, women's soccer. In the college's then 115-year history, the men's team had twice made it to the final rounds of the NCAA championship, while two years before I started at Portland, the women's team had actually won it. In 2002, Clive Charles, the renowned coach and architect of the soccer program at Portland, had taken the Pilots all the way to a 2–1 win in the final round over Santa Clara, a moment of glory the team was desperately trying to repeat. But the last few years had been rough. Charles, a former professional player for West Ham, the English Premier League club, who had coached the US Olympic and Women's National teams, had died of cancer in 2003, and two years later the team was still in flux. The year I joined, the question was whether we could return to the golden age.

I thought we had a good shot. When I looked around the locker room, all I saw were Youth National Team players, including Stephanie Lopez, my old teammate from Elk Grove; Natalie Budge; and Angie Woznuk. By far the best player among us was Christine Sinclair, a senior when I joined the team, in her fifth year of playing for the Pilots and already a regular on the Canadian Women's National Team. She was only two years older than me—twenty-two to my twenty—but her experience so outflanked mine and everyone else's on the team, she was like a woman among girls, and just watching her improved our performance. Christine was a monster that year, scoring something like forty goals over the course of the season—five alone in our second game, against Oregon. After that, we beat San Diego State 3–0, Pacific 2–0, Wisconsin 5–1, West Virginia 2–0, and with the exception of a 1–1 tie with Pepperdine in October, went undefeated the entire season, until we reached the NCAA first round in November.

Those early games I played for the Pilots were thrilling. In some ways, playing for a college team is more intense than playing for a regional or even a national team, because the entire community shares in your fortunes. During a big tournament like the NCAA Women's Soccer Championship, the whole campus lives and breathes soccer in a way I wouldn't experience again until the mania of the 2019 FIFA Women's World Cup in France. A year earlier, the Pilots had been knocked out by Notre Dame in the quarterfinals, and the year before that, lost the tournament title in the third round to Santa Clara. This year was particularly exciting, because we had gone undefeated all season and it felt like a comeback. Finally, we were back on track. All we had to do was hold our nerve.

Easier said than done. In the early rounds, we ground Iowa State into the dust with a 5–0 victory and won a straightforward game against Arizona, in which I scored twice. But once we reached the quarterfinals against Notre Dame, we—particularly the older players—had to work to stay calm. This was when we'd lost to Notre Dame last year. In the team's previous four meetings with Notre Dame, the most successful team in the country after North Carolina, they had won every time. It was hard to not get the jitters.

And the expectations at Portland were running wild. I had played in bigger games in my life, and before bigger crowds, but this was different. There was so much buzz around campus that the game sold out in five minutes. That Friday night in November, when we ran onto the field, it was to cheers so loud, the capacity crowd of five thousand sounded three times that size.

Notre Dame came out strong and in the first twelve minutes completely dominated play. All we could do was ramp up the aggression. In the fourteenth minute, I took an outside shot, smashed from 23 yards, and caught the Notre Dame goalkeeper by surprise. Her hands shot out and she got her fingers to the ball, but it was too late; the ball slammed into the back of the net. Five minutes later, I sent a ball across the goal mouth, forcing the goalkeeper to dive to dismiss it, at which point it found Lindsey Huie, who smacked it in from 15 yards.

Ten minutes later, Notre Dame scored after a

corner kick and we went into halftime with the score at 2–1, not nearly a comfortable enough margin. We were a confident team, but it was clear the game could go either way. Three minutes into the second half, my old friend Stephanie Lopez found me with a perfect pass to the left side of the penalty area, and I made a clean shot: one touch of my right foot, lifting the ball straight over the goalkeeper's head and down into the back of the net: 3–1. It was my second goal of the night, and my thirteenth since my debut in August. A few days later, we would win the semifinal against Penn State on penalties, and a few days after that, the entire tournament, with a 4–0 win against UCLA. Both those games were played at College Station in Texas, and while we were jubilant about winning them and recapturing the title, neither could compare to the game with Notre Dame, played before an ecstatic home crowd.

I knew that night that I loved the drama of the high-stakes game. I knew I had a big-moment gene that allowed me to feed off the energy of the crowd and enjoy the attention; and I knew that I played my best when the pressure was on. When we won 3–1 that night at Merlo Field, we were so over the moon you would think we had won the World Cup.

———

I had made a big splash during my freshman year. In the college sports press, I was referred to as a wunderkind who had "wowed the crowd." ESPN called me a "star" and "world-class talent." My goal tally was almost unprecedented for a freshman, so when I returned as a sophomore, it would be as the leading goal scorer at Portland. (Christine Sinclair, the previous record holder, had graduated that summer and signed with Chelsea, in England, after making generous remarks about me to a reporter: "However she does, the team is going to do," she said. "I think she's that important to them.") At twenty, with that kind of first season under my belt, you can imagine what I was like: head swelled, feeling great, going into my second season pretty much thinking, I'm awesome. And then Greg Ryan, the USWNT coach, called to invite me onto the national team.

If anything could bring me down to size, it was walking into the national team locker room as the youngest and least experienced player. In May 2006, I joined the senior team at a residential training camp in LA, and felt like I was stepping into a dream. There was Kate Markgraf, veteran World Cup player. There was Aly Wagner, a national team veteran. The person I was most wowed by was Kristine Lilly, a complete legend who by the end of her playing career in 2010 would be the most capped player—clocking 354 games for the US team—in the history of the sport. She and Kate had both played in the 1999 FIFA World Cup–winning team, which meant that as a teenager I had spent hours staring at their faces on my wall. I couldn't quite believe I was here.

Kristine was a particular inspiration to me. She was cool, kind, and unpretentious, but what most thrilled me about her was the fact that she was only five foot four. That someone so slight had risen to the top of the game—through skills rather than brute strength—was hugely encouraging to me, as was her reputation for being an unselfish player.

Two months later, I was put on the roster for my first national team game, a friendly against Ireland in San Diego, and if training camp had been exciting, this was momentous. I'm low-key about most things. When I play, it's with the attitude that it's great to win and OK to lose. Suddenly, however, I was nervous. Losing my first national game would suck. The history of pro soccer is littered with national team tryouts who played one game and were never invited back, and I definitely didn't want to be one of those. In early July, I downscaled my twenty-first birthday celebrations because I had practice the next day, canceled everything else in my calendar to focus on training, and three weeks later, walked out onto the field.

When you're surrounded by players who are much, much better than you, your performance improves. It's easy to be good when everyone around you is good. There are no bad passes, no missed shots. Every opportunity you're given is golden. Playing on a less talented team can actually be a better test of your skill, when you're doing the work of three people. But as a young player, working for the first time in tandem with the best players in the world felt like being in a different game altogether.

That day in San Diego, I ran out alongside titans of the game, including Abby Wambach, Heather O'Reilly, and Christie Welsh. They treated me the way I try to treat younger players now, which was with kindness and seriousness, and not too much fussing. No one can hand-hold you into a great performance, and you want young players to be free and wild. At the same time, you want them to understand they are entering an established professional culture, where the older players set the standard. On the field, the veterans looked me in the eye and, without saying anything explicit, let me know this was another level and I had to hit the ground running. Along with Carli Lloyd and Stephanie Lopez, the other new players, I watched their intensity and commitment, and set about copying them.

The US battered Ireland 5–0 that day, and while I didn't score, I played well enough to be immediately reselected for a friendly a few weeks later against Canada, and then for the penultimate friendly of the season, a game in LA against Chinese Taipei. Finally, I scored my first goal for the national team: two, in fact, contributing to a 10–0 win (Carli scored her first international goal in that game, too) over our rivals. It was October 2006, almost a year to the day before the 2007 FIFA World Cup was due to take place, and in November the team would fly to South Korea for the qualifying rounds. I felt sure I had a shot at being included.

A week later, I was scheduled to play with the Pilots in a home game against Washington State. It was a low-key Thursday-night match and the contrast was a little head spinning. I had gone directly from playing in a 27,000-seat stadium with the best players in the world to a 5,000-seat field in Portland with a bunch of other college kids. The change of pressure and pace was a relief honestly, and after the whistle blew, I relaxed into the game. Toward the end of the first half, we were two goals up (one scored by Rachael in the twenty-ninth minute) and looking good to keep on dominating the game. Just before halftime, I ran to block a pass, planted my left foot on the turf, and after feeling a sting in my knee, suddenly found myself down on the field.

I wasn't in pain. This wasn't a contact injury, so there was no trauma, and it didn't seem to me to be a big deal—which is what I always think about things that turn out to be a big deal. That evening, when the doctor told me I'd torn my anterior cruciate ligament, a common knee injury in soccer, or any sport that requires sudden changes of speed and direction, I was pretty relaxed. I was told I'd need surgery the following week and would miss out on playing with the national team in a friendly against Iceland that Sunday. But my meniscus wasn't torn and I wasn't in agony. Besides which, I was twenty-one years old and clearly invincible.

Being injured puts you in a weird limbo. You have to keep training to maintain your fitness, without working toward the fixed goal of a game. Rehab is double the work of regular training, and to get back up to your level, you're in the gym early and out late, which can be lonely and demoralizing. Some coaches ask injured players to attend practice and watch from the sidelines, which seemed to me a recipe for depression and which I avoided. The best way to move forward, I decided, was to get better in record time, and rejoin practice with my invincibility restored.

The early days after the injury weren't really that bad. But as the days became weeks, and weeks became months, it became clear this was a bigger problem than anticipated. I missed the qualifiers in South Korea. I missed all the games in the NCAA tournament that season. (Portland lost in the quarterfinals against UCLA.) I ended up playing only ten games in my sophomore year, and as the 2007 season got under way without me, it looked as if I would spend even less time on the field as a junior. I started to feel out of sorts.

In early September, with one eye on the World Cup coming up in November, I pushed myself as hard as I could. After swearing to the coach I was ready to come back, I appeared in two games for the Pilots that fall, one against Cal State Fullerton on September 7, and one against Purdue two days later. Both were disastrous. I lasted thirteen minutes in the first game; and although I played for most of the second half against Purdue, I wasn't remotely in form. A few weeks later, during a training session, I felt my knee ping. I had torn my ACL again.

It was enraging and frustrating, and I could hardly believe it had happened. Ridiculously, Rachael had just done exactly the same thing, on the same knee, and a year later would do it again. In short order it went me, her, me, her, so that in October 2007 we both found ourselves in the position of needing a knee operation. I hadn't liked my previous surgeon, and after doing some research, our mom found Dr. Michael Dillingham, a former NFL team doctor for the 49ers, who would see us in San Francisco.

ACL knee surgery is fiddly. They take the

ligament out and use a skin graft to repair it. Then they drill holes in the heads of your tibia and femur, put the repaired ligament back in, and pin it in place with a screw. A lot of people use skin from their arms for the graft, but I was too small, so they used cadaver grafts instead. The surgery took a couple of hours. When I came round, my mom was sitting by my bed.

"You know, Megan," she said, "it's not the end of the world. You still have your college scholarship, and you've achieved great things already."

I knew what she was trying to say. Two injuries on the same knee within the space of a year was a good indication your career was wrecked, and my mom wasn't the only one to think so. Within days of my injury, career obituaries started running in the college press, in which my ambitions were referred to exclusively in the past tense. "Rapinoe was also making a push to be a regular on the United States Women's National Team," ran one. Clearly, everyone thought I was done.

I couldn't blame them; I had busted my ACL twice in a row, why wouldn't they think that? And while I was lucky that, in the days after the surgery, I was healing well and wouldn't need a further operation, I would have to stay in San Francisco for rehab, which was gruesome. Years later, I would discover that Sue Bird, my girl-friend, had the same physical therapist as Rachael and I did—Lisa, Dr. Dillingham's wife, and the toughest PT we ever had. It was a house of pain, more hard-core than any training I've ever done for the national team, to the extent that I still do some of the exercises and squats she taught us today.

In the weeks after surgery, I was quieter than usual. I may not have shut myself in my room, as I used to when I was a kid, and I didn't drink or take drugs or go off the rails. But Rachael says this time was the most dispirited she'd ever seen me. I was helpless, with no sense of purpose and no one to blame but myself. Rachael was in bad shape after her injury, too, but her ambitions had changed and she hadn't been banking on a career on the national team. For me, recovery was deeply frustrating. To know I could compete at the highest level and to be prevented from doing so was awful, and I had no back-up plan. I'd never so much as had a job before, not even when we were kids, when our parents had said as long as we were working hard at what we loved, they would take care of the rest. Well, all I loved was soccer and now I couldn't play.

Slowly, regular life resumed. In between rehab, PT, and training, I went back to being a normal student. I studied, hung out, drank too much in the spring, went to class. I was dating someone and thought I might be in love. Rachael and I left the campus dorms and moved into a big house with a bunch of other students, before moving out again, fast. (My sister is super fastidious and I'm a borderline slob, but even for me the house was too wild. We got an apartment together and were much happier.) I was low, for sure. But I took one day at a time. And while it was painful, in August, to watch the Olympic Games on TV, at least I was out of action long before team selection took place. If I'd made the Olympic squad and been cut, the experience would've been much harder. When the USA won gold, I didn't think, I could have been there.

I wasn't going to make the same mistake twice. This time, I was determined to go slow and heal properly. I was going to learn patience and humility and accept that however good I was, I wasn't invincible. Stripped of its delusions, my ambition grew stronger. When I'd woken up from surgery that day and my mom had tried to console me, I'd had the strongest feeling I didn't need consolation. "Mom," I said, "I'm not done."

7

CHICAGO

When I met Abby Wambach in 2006, she was the star of the national team. I was twenty-one, in my sophomore year at college, and had just started training alongside her. She was five years older than me and already a veteran of international games. We began dating almost immediately, and although as my first serious relationship it was almost by definition guaranteed to fail, the experience was intense. I really loved her.

Being a professional athlete can be hard on your personal life, but in the early days with Abby, the fact that we were rarely in the same town was a plus. Every time she came to see me in Portland, the honeymoon period rebooted. I suffered the first ACL injury a few months after we met, and the prolonged excitement of a long-distance relationship was a welcome distraction from rehab, as was the fact that in the relatively small world of women's professional soccer, Abby was a celebrity. She would fly into town for a few days, we would hang out and have a great time, and she would leave again before things got too real. If there was no will-you-go-to-the-store-to-buy-milk, or pressure for the relationship to engage with the nitty-gritty of life, I was 100 percent down for that. Apart from anything else, it allowed me to preserve all my energy for recovery.

I trained hard all through 2007 and the first half of 2008 without playing a single game. In the spring of my senior year, I began to feel fit again, and that August, I returned to the Pilots lineup. The first game of the season was at home against Oregon, and I wasn't nervous. I had waited so long and been so conscientious about rehab that I felt pretty confident running out onto the field. I made four shots on goal that night, and ran almost from one end of the field to the other before crossing to a teammate, who smashed it in. Two of Portland's three goals were scored off my assists, and after the game, when the coach set off fireworks to celebrate the start of the season, I felt as if they were personally for me. I was back.

My comeback was great in terms of my career. I hadn't returned to the national team yet, but I was performing better than ever, helping the Pilots to a nineteen-game winning streak that year, which took us to the NCAA semifinals. (We lost 1–0 to Stanford in that game—not a bad result given we were missing four of our best players, three of them to the Under-20 National Team at the World Cup in Chile, and Rachael, who had reinjured her tendon.) My life seemed to be getting back to normal.

Or at least it did professionally. Emerging from two years of limbo was a pretty big life change, one that brought to the forefront certain aspects of my relationship with Abby. Five years is a big age gap when you're dating in college, and at twenty-two, after two years on the bench, I was fresh and raring to go. Abby, on the other hand, was entering a tough midcareer phase. In July 2008, she broke her leg in a match just before the Olympics. The injury was bad, and she was understandably an emotional wreck, but I found myself recoiling from her needs. I was free and happy for the first time in years and I didn't want to be pulled into someone else's problems. I had no idea what to do.

Looking back, what I see is two young people who for a while were deeply in love. I also see the selfishness of youth. At the time, Abby seemed so much older than me that I gave her almost no leeway to make mistakes, or have needs. Now, of course, I realize that she was young, too, only twenty-five when we met and still figuring things out. When she broke her leg, I was impatient and unsympathetic, and immature enough to want to get out to avoid having to deal with it.

In the end it was my sister who called it. Rachael and I generally give each other space to date whomever we want, but we can also look each other in the eye and say, It's fucking **over**, you have to move on. She and my mom liked Abby. But one night, while we were sitting around on campus, my sister said, You have to break up with her. I looked at her, eyes wide, head nodding. The timing was bad and ours was an unceremonious ending—I basically left Abby in the hospital bed with her broken leg—but my sister was right.

I hadn't played for the national team in over two years, but by the end of 2008, I was playing so well I knew the phone call was probably coming. In the meantime, there were new opportunities. In January 2009, I had to make a choice. I could either graduate from Portland and accept a job playing for the Chicago Red Stars, who had selected me second overall in the 2009 Women's Professional Soccer draft. (The first pick in the draft was Amy Rodriguez, who went to the Boston Breakers.)

Or I could redo my senior year. I'd missed so much playing time at Portland that per the terms of my scholarship, I qualified for a redshirt year. However, after all those years of sitting around, I was ready for my life to begin. I was gracious, of course, and thanked everyone who'd helped me at Portland. But I was also young and impatient, and desperate to move on. I will see you fucking later, I thought.

The history of women's soccer leagues is a history of failed enterprise, underinvestment, small crowds, and big disappointments, as well as women playing for little or no money. The first-ever league, which started playing in 2001, grew out of the success of the 1999 FIFA Women's World Cup–winning team, and was called the Women's United Soccer Association. WUSA had eight teams. It folded in 2003, after three seasons. Six years later the Women's Professional Soccer league, comprised of seven teams, was formed in its place, and was set up on the back of the national team winning gold at the 2008 Olympics. In March 2009, I moved to Chicago to play for the Red Stars in the WPS inaugural season. Along with everyone else, I hoped this was the league that would last.

I didn't know Chicago at all, but because of the way player housing was organized, living and playing there was a lot like being back in college. The entire team, including Carli Lloyd and Lindsay Tarpley, captain of the Red Stars, was housed in a single apartment block in the downtown neighborhood of Streeterville, with a bar on the ground floor of the building. We put in a lot of hours in that bar. Rachael came to see me and my parents visited, and those first few weeks flew by like a whirlwind. We had a blast.

There was one big difference between being a student and being in Chicago, of course, and that was money. At college, I'd gotten by on a combination of my scholarship, contributions from my parents, and small stipends from the National Olympic Committee for being on the national team. Now, for the first time in my life, I was earning. I was on a WPS player salary of around thirty-two thousand dollars, and that March I also signed a contract with the national team and was put on a tier 2 salary of fifty thousand dollars a year, with the possibility, if I hit tier 1, of my salary increasing to around seventy thousand dollars. I had nothing to compare my salary to and I didn't think to question it. The number seemed perfectly adequate to me, and immediately after signing, I flew to Portugal with the team to compete in the Algarve Cup, a low-key international tournament of twelve teams. The crowds in Portugal were tiny—we lost the final game against Sweden in front of 1,200 people—but returning to the national team was intense after my years on the bench. Soccer had always been front and center, but now, with no classes, no distractions, and no other demands

on my time, it wasn't just my passion, it was my
job. This was life as a professional athlete.

In the beginning, at least, I felt this transition
more keenly at the league level. National games
were a much bigger deal and the real measure
of my career, but they were also sporadically organized and subject to busy tournament schedules interspersed with long down periods. Life in
the league, on the other hand, was much more
nine-to-five. The Red Stars' home ground was a
28,000-seat stadium about twelve miles southwest of downtown, and the training schedule,
once I returned from Portugal, was like nothing
I'd experienced before. I wasn't lazy. But I was inconsistent and had, until then, the supreme confidence of the young that you could float through
training sessions and make up for it later. Back in
August 2006, when I'd started playing for the
national team, the coach, Greg Ryan, had said
something sharp about my training habits. He'd
called me "one of the most creative young players
in the national system," before saying he'd noticed
I had an aversion to practice. He wasn't wrong. I
look back now and think, Oh, what a mess. I was
so unprofessional. In the middle of the season,
I'd still go out and have a couple of beers at dinner or stay out late. If I wanted a burger, I'd have
one, and although I was generally quite healthy,
there was no rhyme or reason to any of my habits.

I didn't understand that training is what gets you into the game, that it's the difference between winning and losing, and for a long time I was not a great training player. I was fit enough to get away with it, but looking back, I wish I'd been better.

Playing on a daily basis forced me to improve, and those league games with the Red Stars were where I really started to sharpen my skills. Playing at club level is hard. If you're a national team member, you're likely one of the best players on your league team, which means that your opponents will zone in on you. During those early games in Chicago, I would ask myself: How many goals can I manufacture basically by myself? How do I find a way to be impactful and to make other players better? I learned how to play with greater consistency. I learned how to be in the right place at the right time. When players get described as "creative," as I often do, the meaning varies depending on who's saying it and why. Sometimes when I see a player called "creative" I think, No, they're just doing a bunch of stupid tricks, like step overs or scissors, that have no effect on the game. I don't do a lot of that stuff. My strengths are simple: I can use both feet, I have good vision, and I like to play quickly. I'm never going to be dribbling, dribbling, dribbling. That's not me at all, and I'm not good at it.

I think back to what I'd learned as a kid, which

was how to be successful without being physically the best. My creativity comes out in my vision and in my passing ability, in the fact that I'm willing to try things and fail. Taking a calculated risk and being a little unpredictable fall under the banner of creativity, as does knowing the game really well. As my training improved, I tried to find opportunities—an unexpected cross, a long pass up the field to someone so out of range no one was paying attention to them—before other players did.

We didn't have a great season. There were a lot of brilliant players on the Red Stars, but we had a young, inexperienced coach and for some reason we never meshed as a team. After winning our first game in April against Saint Louis Athletica, we basically lost or tied ten games in a row. Our longest winning streak was two games against Washington Freedom and the California team FC Gold Pride, and we finished the season in second-to-last place. I was doing well on the national team, having been in the starting lineup for six games that year and ending the season leading the team in points, but the failure in Chicago was still disappointing.

There was one bright spot toward the end of the year. In the fall of 2009, I was introduced by a Red Stars teammate to Sarah, an Australian forward for Sky Blue FC, a league team in Harrison, New Jersey. If every new relationship is, to some small degree, a correction to the one that came before, then Sarah was just what I needed. She was relaxed, very cool, and with a spunky personality. Australians can be known to be a little corny, but Sarah was hilarious, and as the season finished up and we headed into winter, we tried to spend as much time together as we could.

At Christmas, all the players in the league scattered. Sarah headed back to Sydney to play for the Australian national team during winter break, and I returned to my parents' house in Redding. I was twenty-four, and I felt like a teenager all over again. My sister, who had taken a redshirt year at Portland and had just graduated, was home, too, so we were back to sharing our old bedroom. Brian was off doing his thing. Austin was almost ten, and at school. After graduating, CeCé had married her high school sweetheart, Donnie—which Rachael and I had been lobbying for since we were five years old—and was raising a family in Redding, and Jenny was married and working locally, too. My dad still pulled long hours in construction, and my mom was still working at Jack's. The day after I got home, I woke up and came down the hallway to find my mom sitting in her chair in her dressing gown, hair wild, drinking coffee, ruling the morning as she had done all my life.

Returning to the same fixed point allows you

to measure how far you've gone and that's what it was like coming home. The day after I arrived, I headed to downtown Redding and my old gym at the YMCA. Walking through the familiar sliding doors was bizarre. I remembered working out in this gym as a teenager. Now I was swiping in and saying hi to the desk clerk as a player on the national team. I wasn't exactly a big shot. I hadn't played in a World Cup, or been to the Olympics, and no one beyond my family and a few hardcore fans knew who I was. Still, the transformation seemed to me like an improbable leap. My only goal as a kid had been to keep playing the sport I loved, and it had brought me here, to a career playing for my country alongside the best in the world. I was incredulous.

The sensation didn't last long. One benefit of our noisy household was the impossibility of holding on to romantic notions about yourself without someone loudly shutting them down. "What do you think?" I asked Rachael that night, about an outfit I was thinking of wearing to Jack's. She looked up from the bed. "Trash," she said, and even though I was irritated, I knew she was right. On Christmas Eve, our mom did her famous buffet for the family, which thirty-plus members turned up for, including most of my mom's siblings and their spouses and kids. And although everyone asked eagerly about my life as a player, soccer and its anxieties suddenly seemed far away. There was no social media in those days, and I had almost no public profile. But I began to realize that Christmas was something that would become even more important to me in subsequent years—whatever happened out there, real life was here.

Rachael's second ACL injury hadn't finished her career as a player, and in the new year, while she was figuring out what she wanted to do in the long term, she moved to Iceland to play for the team, Stjarnan Women. I headed back to Chicago and new digs in Bucktown, which was a much funkier neighborhood than Streeterville. Sarah had been traded to a team in St. Louis, and it would be a busy few months, juggling my playing schedule for the Red Stars with training camps for the national team, and traveling to see Sarah in Missouri.

There was a joke rule of thumb on the team. Because so many of the players were in the closet or trying to hide their sexuality, the benchmark was, basically, that if you flew to see someone on your day off, there was no way you weren't sleeping with them. People would be, like, Oh, I'm just going to visit a friend in California, and we'd exchange glances and call bullshit. If you get on a plane on your off day, when you're exhausted and just want to rest, you're having sex. That's just the bottom line.

I was out to everyone on the team and I was

out to my family, and beyond that, no one was asking. The average attendance for a Red Stars home game was four thousand—pretty small— but even the national team wasn't that popular, and no one outside the locker room was speculating about our personal lives. I wasn't naive about the difficulties of being a gay person in sports; there was a reason none of the big stars were out. And growing up in Redding, I wasn't deluded about homophobia in small towns or religious communities. But beyond that, I hadn't given my being gay much thought. I truly believed, in the spring of 2010, that I had done all the coming out I would need to.

Marriage equality had been in and out of the news for a few years at that point. In 2008, only two states permitted same-sex marriage— Massachusetts and California—although just as quickly as the law had been passed in California, it had been revoked under Proposition 8. In 2009, a federal lawsuit had been filed challenging Prop 8, and in 2010, a judge had declared the ban in violation of the equal protection clause. The case had started making its way through the appeals process toward the Supreme Court, just as another high profile case hit the news.

Edith Windsor was an indefatigable campaigner for gay rights. In 2009, Thea Spyer, her partner of over forty years, had died, and although the couple had been legally married in Canada, their marriage wasn't recognized by the federal government in the US. After Spyer's death, Windsor was hit with estate taxes in the hundreds of thousands that she would have had written off as a spousal deduction if she had been the surviving spouse in a heterosexual couple. In 2010, at the age of eighty, she filed a lawsuit against the federal government, claiming that the definition of "spouse" in this context—that is, as exclusive to marriages between men and women—was unconstitutional. In both the challenge to Proposition 8 and Edith Windsor's lawsuit, the Supreme Court was years away from making a ruling. But the publicity around the cases was huge.

Reading about what was going on triggered a visceral reaction. Marriage equality was a personal issue to me, and as I watched **United States v. Windsor** work its way through the courts and read the commentary about the debate, I understood that these cases weren't isolated. They were expressions of an injustice that was baked into the system, and that would take a huge clamor to change. As a kid, I'd always pushed back against bullies and stood up for myself and my friends. Now, as an adult, I felt something dormant in me twitching to life: political anger.

8

THE ONLY GAY ON
THE TEAM

I don't really do risk assessment, at least not in the traditional sense. If I'm thinking of doing or saying something that might potentially cause trouble, I don't base my decision on how it might land. Instead, the three questions I ask myself are: (a) Do I believe in what I'm saying? (b) Do I know that what I'm saying is right? And (c) Does it need to be said as a matter of urgency? If the answer to all three is yes, I don't have anything else to decide. I might avoid an issue if I don't feel strongly about it or am underinformed, but otherwise I'm getting involved. In 2010, the campaign for marriage equality inflamed and informed me. In 2011, the popularity of my team during the World Cup in Germany gave me a platform that compelled me to act.

In the run-up to the tournament, I didn't think the 2011 FIFA World Cup would be different from any other big competition in US women's soccer history, which is to say we would probably do very well, there'd be a flurry of press interest, then the attention would die down and our lives would go back to normal. It had been this way ever since the team's first big win in 1999, when the US victory at the World Cup had failed to translate into better ticket sales year-round. Every four years, people get excited about women's soccer, then for reasons no one can fathom or control, interest fizzles out. This was the way things were and, we were led to believe, would always be.

In the fall of 2010, we blazed through the early rounds of the CONCACAF World Cup qualifying matches—the FIFA regional tournament organized by the Confederation of North, Central American, and Caribbean Association Football, which took place alongside those of five other regions—achieving the kind of lopsided results we were accustomed to as number one in the world: 9–0 against Guatemala, 5–0 Haiti, and so on until we'd racked up nineteen victories in a row. In the semifinals, we suffered an upset. Mexico hadn't qualified for the World Cup since 1999, when they'd come in last and the US had won, and that night in Cancún, they were ranked twenty-one places below us. The crowd of eight thousand people was boisterously behind them, and to our shock, Mexico scored in the third minute. Carli Lloyd equalized twenty-three minutes later, but we never got back on track. My play was choppy and inconsistent and my shots on goal all went high, and we finished the game trailing 2–1. The crowd was so psyched that clearly many of them thought we were out of the World Cup. In fact, we still managed to qualify by beating Costa Rica a few days later, then Italy in the CONCACAF-UEFA match. But it was a bumpy road, and when the press called our defeat by Mexico "the greatest upset in women's soccer history," they weren't a million miles from the truth. (Although perhaps that said less about our performance than the brevity of women's soccer history.)

At home, the Chicago Red Stars were having another bad season. For two years in a row now we had finished second to last in the league, and after the drama in Mexico, I was ready for a break. I'd hardly seen Sarah in months, and at the end of the year, after spending Christmas together in Redding, we headed to Australia for winter break. Spending a few weeks in the sun before coming home in the new year seemed like the perfect vacation, and I wouldn't even fall behind in my training. During the US off-season, Sarah played with her Aussie league team, Sydney FC, and I tagged along to train with them. The trip was exactly what I needed, and at the end of January, I was ready to return, refreshed, to the US.

On the plane to California, I started to feel strange. I was flying to Redding via LA to visit my family. At first I just had a headache. It got worse over the course of the flight, until it was so bad I thought my head would explode. Then I started to ache and feel nauseous. My dad picked me up at the airport in Redding, and when I got home, I collapsed into bed. A few days later, I couldn't get up and the doctor was called. I had meningitis. It wasn't the bacterial kind that can kill you, but it was pretty severe, and I was laid up for the best part of a month. I was extremely fortunate this coincided with the off-season, but even so, it took everything I had to get back on my feet, and my mother has never recovered. Even now, ten years later, she'll still say, "Are you OK? You sound tired," and I'll know from the strain in her voice that she's thinking back to the meningitis. ("Mom, of course I'm tired," I'll say. "I'm a professional athlete; it's **literally my job** to be tired.")

At twenty-five, I was young and fit enough to bounce back relatively quickly, and I was heavily incentivized. My first-ever World Cup was five months away, and having missed out four years earlier thanks to my ACL injury, I was determined to be ready this time. But it was a shaky start to the year. In the months before the competition, the performance of the national team was up and down—in March, we were in the final of the Algarve Cup, and I was in good form, scoring an early goal against Japan in the opening rounds and the winning goal against Norway that got us into the final. A few weeks later we lost to England, which was a blow. Still, I was feeling pretty confident, and in May, when Pia Sundhage, the team coach, announced the World Cup roster, I knew I deserved my place on the team.

I liked Pia. She wasn't everyone's cup of tea, but no coach ever is, given that they always need to leave someone on the bench. Pia could be a little inflexible, and she wasn't always the best communicator, but as a person she was funny and eccentric, and we had a good working relationship. That June, the team geared up to fly to the World Cup in Germany. We played our farewell match against Mexico in New Jersey, to a dispiritingly small crowd of 8,000 people in a 25,000-seat stadium, lest any of us harbored delusions about the popularity of women's soccer. Then we got on the plane to Germany. Right before the tournament began, Pia took me aside and told me I wouldn't be in the starting lineup for the first game against North Korea. I had lost my spot to Lauren Cheney, who was two years younger than me and had competed in the 2008 Olympics in Beijing. I was pissed.

I don't tend to internalize other people's feelings

toward me. I'm so self-critical and honest when I mess up that when I feel confident about something, I tend to think that it's justified. I had only been playing for the national team for two years and was among the less experienced players on the roster, which included veterans such as Christie Rampone, Shannon Boxx, and Abby, with whom I'd patched up enough of a friendship to assuage any awkwardness. And I understood that Pia was under a lot of pressure going into the World Cup. But I had scored a lot of goals during the CONCACAF qualifying rounds, as well as set up Amy Rodriguez's goal in the game against Italy that got us through to the World Cup. I had also played well in Portugal. Perhaps that hadn't been enough and there wasn't a huge case to be made. But being benched was a real blow.

When I know I'm being underestimated, my performance improves. What are you going to do? The only recourse is to double down and play so well no one can doubt you again. When we got to Dresden, the excitement of being at the World Cup was intensified by my excitement about getting on the field and proving myself. The opening game against North Korea gave me almost no opportunities—I came on late in the second half and we won a businesslike 2–0—but our second game against Colombia was different.

I came out at halftime and almost immediately scored, a clean strike from inside the penalty area, which felt like the purest retort to Pia. I wasn't the only one who saw it that way. "There's an answer to the coach!" screamed the English commentator on ESPN, and the camera flashed to Pia high-fiving the assistant coaches. Over the years, I had heard a lot of talk about what being an athlete was about, a lot of it bullshit about the purity of the game. Now I had an answer of my own: as a professional soccer player, there is nothing like being screamed at by twenty-five thousand people after scoring a goal in the World Cup to confirm that you work in a branch of entertainment. After scoring, I grabbed a sideline mic that was lying on the edge of the pitch, and with Lauren Cheney and Lori Lindsey at my side, Lindsey on air guitar on the other, busted out a line from "Born in the U.S.A." The crowd went wild.

I had a lot of family in the crowd that day, not only my parents and Rachael, but also my aunt Melanie and her daughters, Aleta and Anna, all of whom stayed throughout the tournament and cheered me on the whole way. A few days later, we lost to Sweden, an upset for sure but not enough to stop us advancing to the quarterfinals, and that's when we ran up against Brazil. It's strange to be able to date a new phase of one's life to a particular moment, but there's no question, looking back, that the fortunes of the national team—as a brand and as a team—changed definitively that day. Going in, all we knew was that the game was

likely to be dramatic. We had a long history of rivalry with Brazil and it was personal. Their reputation for bad sportsmanship was deserved and
annoying, and when they started acting poorly in
Dresden that night, the crowd, initially on their
side, started to turn against them. By the final
whistle, we had tied 1–1 and went into stoppage
time with what felt like all twenty-five thousand
people on our side.

Up to that point, the whole game had been
kind of weird, choppy, and uneven, with neither
side really finding its rhythm. We had scored
early on—or, rather, Brazil had scored an own
goal—and then we'd almost immediately been
given a red card. Brazil had taken a penalty and
missed it, been given a do-over, and scored. A few
minutes into stoppage time, they scored again,
putting them ahead 2–1. We were down to ten
players because of the red card. The fight was on.

I've heard rival players, particularly from
Europe, talk about the US as an unbeatable team
because of our "winning mentality." We lose, of
course. I've won plenty and lost plenty. The difference is that we truly believe we're going to win,
in every single game, no matter how the game
is going or at what stage it's in. In a country of
330 million people, only 23 women get to make
a living the way we do, and you need to be a
gladiator just to get on the team. You're in the
cauldron every day. We train to win, and we play

to win, and every second of play we're relentless. Sweden has a good mentality. Japan before 2015 was pretty cutthroat. The old German team had that outlook for sure. But not all teams think this way, and it's the difference between winning and losing.

In the 122nd minute, I was thinking, We're fucked. But I can hold two thoughts in my head at one time, and while thinking, We're fucked—because we're in the dying minutes of the game, the ball is way down on our end, and the Brazilians are trying to run down the clock with their antics—I'm also seeing Ali Krieger dribbling up the sideline, passing the ball to the middle to Carli, and then Carli dribbling for what seems like an eternity. And I'm like, Just fucking pass the ball to me! Because I'm open and coming up on the left! And she dribbles across the field, finally plays it; I take one touch, and I don't even really look up. But I'm like, Bitch, you'd better be there. **Somebody** has to be there. And it was literally a Hail Mary pass. This was our last chance—the ref should already have blown the whistle—and I just bombed it up the field, where the ball found Abby, who headed it in. "Oh my god!" she screamed. "Oh my god! Best cross of your life!"

"I know!" I screamed back. We were back from the dead and over the moon.

People always ask me: Did you see Abby in

that moment? And the answer is, no, it was a moment of pure desperation. I just fucking smashed the ball with my left foot and hoped for the best. On the other hand, yes, I did "see" her to the extent that I've been working on this my whole life. I know how to put myself in the right position to throw all my might behind a final push. My right foot is better and more accurate than my left, but I work on my left foot all the time. I work on it so hard it becomes second nature, so that when I need to call on it in a moment like this, I'm not thinking, Can I even put the ball up there? I just do it.

It was an epic sports moment, extremely dramatic. I imagined people back home watching, sitting in bars, jumping up to celebrate when the whistle blew. We were tied 2–2 and the game went to a penalty shootout, which we won 5–3. If we'd lost, it would have been a catastrophic exit from the World Cup—our earliest ever, with no medal rounds, nothing—and after it was all over, we collapsed with something we rarely feel as a team: overwhelming relief.

That clip of my cross to Abby and her stupendous header into the goal went what we didn't yet know to call viral. It jumped from ESPN to all the mainstream news and talk shows. It was endlessly played and discussed in the media. We were still in a bubble, going from hotel, to field, to ESPN studio, but we knew something had

broken through. Friends and family started calling us. Then we started to see numbers. The average global TV audience for the World Cup so far
was 13 million per game, across 181 countries, a
huge increase from previous World Cups. After
we got through the semis against France 3–1, it
rose to 62 million for the final. In America, audience reach had increased by almost 200 percent
over the previous World Cup, peaking for the
final at 14 million.

These numbers were mind-boggling, and not
just because we had played well. One of the reasons audience figures were up in the US was because during the 2007 World Cup, matches had
been scheduled to air in the morning, so no one
had been able to watch. This time around, they
were aired throughout the day and after work.
I could see now that there were specific ways of
inflating or depressing people's engagement with
women's soccer, rather than, as I had understood
to be the case, interest in us waxing and waning
as if it were a natural phenomenon, like weather.

The final against Japan was a nail-biter. Four
months earlier, Japan had suffered a catastrophic
tsunami that had killed fifteen thousand people.
If ever a nation needed some joy, they did. We
played hard, edged into the lead with a low strike
from Alex Morgan, surrendered our lead, then
squandered a bunch of goal opportunities so that
by the final whistle we were tied 2–2. Abby scored

in overtime and we were celebrating like crazy until Japan equalized, and once again the game went to a penalty shootout. To lose in the final of the World Cup is agonizing. To lose 1–3 on penalties is almost unbearable.

We were crushed. We were also, however, saved from the worst of the disappointment by the energy around the World Cup. Almost immediately, we realized that something about this tournament had been different; the buzz around our return was huge. This was the first Twitter World Cup—the platform had only been a year old in 2007 and no one had been using it. By 2011, although I still couldn't imagine a day when, to pick a random example, the president of the United States might use Twitter as his primary method of address, the social media service had become popular enough for us to feel the spike in engagement. Here was the beginning of our social media life, and it was thrilling. People bandied around stats like "seven thousand tweets a second" to describe fans reacting to us online while we played. It was at that point, while we were letting this sink in and wondering what would happen when we got home, when I started to feel uncomfortable.

On the plane on the way back from Germany, we were all in pretty bad moods. Our bodies were trashed. We'd gotten totally drunk the night before flying. And now I had one of the worst fucking seats on the flight—first row of economy, nowhere to put my feet, and the table didn't come out. I had Alex Morgan on one side and Lori Lindsey on the other, and Dan, my agent, was sitting behind me. At some point I turned to Lori and said, "This is just dumb."

We had been talking about the way athletes never come out, particularly when the spotlight is on them. I'd never been in the spotlight before. The team hadn't been popular enough. Now, as we flew back into the eye of a media storm, we were popular and I didn't feel right. "This is weird, right?" I said to Lori, who is one of my best friends and had been feeling weird, too. "Yup," she said.

All year I'd been reading about gay rights and the law, and it had made me much more politically aware. Coming out, I understood now, was not a zero sum game, but more of a process. I wasn't in the closet, but no one in the press knew I was gay and that aspect of my life wasn't part of the conversation. Saying something now might be impactful—I don't think I used those kinds of words yet, but I was making my way toward that conclusion. "Clearly this is a public issue and we're public figures," I said to Lori, but it wasn't only that. Not talking about my sexuality felt intuitively bad, like I was operating a policy of don't ask, don't tell, or flying deliberately under the radar. "I'm gay, and an athlete, and I just want to be out," I said. I looked down the aircraft at all the other gay players, most of them older than me. Why am I not out? I thought, impatiently. Why are we all not out?

I swung around in my seat to talk to Dan. Once a decision feels right, I don't agonize or have reservations. I felt similar to the way I had when I came out to my parents, which was that (a) people were not going to be surprised to find out I was gay. And (b) if this **was** going to be a super big deal to people, then that's wack, and they're not going to be in my life anyway. But the way the world was going, I didn't think this was going to be a problem. Being a professional athlete, particularly if you're female, is not like being a Hollywood star, where your sexuality has a bearing on the way people perceive your performance. I had never struggled with accepting this part of myself, so there was no hitch when it came to telling other people.

Dan was supportive from the jump. He wasn't just cool with my plan, he actively encouraged it and never raised a single alarm about potential commercial damages, or told me to slow down and give the decision some thought. Instead, he was a real cheerleader just when I needed one, and I will always be grateful to him. I wasn't going to blurt it out on **Jimmy Fallon** that night.

But by the time we flew to London the following year for the 2012 Olympics, I decided I would be fully, publicly out.

There was no reception committee for us when we landed at JFK, but when the team bus arrived in New York and parked in front of the W hotel, a crowd of people and media had gathered outside. It was wild. For the next few days, we were plunged into an intense PR schedule, getting up at the crack of dawn to shoot the morning shows, and staying up until well after midnight to appear on the late-night shows. On the street, everyone wanted to stop us and talk. I don't tend to think of tournaments in theatrical terms, but the story of the World Cup—my cross to Abby in the dying moments of the quarters, and the extraordinary finale of Japan winning after the tsunami—had captured the country's imagination. We rebranded our victory tour a "welcome home" tour and played three exhibition matches, and everywhere we went there was commotion and excitement. "This is so bizarre," I said at one point on the bus, "but it feels like we won the World Cup!" To which Christie Rampone, the team captain who had played on multiple Olympic gold medal–winning squads, whipped around and snapped, "No it doesn't." She was right. One of the biggest dangers of being number one in the world is complacency. We hadn't won. We were overcelebrating.

Slowly the fuss around us started to die down, and as we scattered back to our league teams, it felt like the right time—not at the height of the post–World Cup media frenzy, but with the lead-up to London 2012 under way—to follow through with the decision I had made on the way back from Germany. After spending the winter break in Australia with Sarah, I got back to the US and scheduled an interview with **Out** magazine. I'd been talking to Rachael, and she was gung ho on my side. And I'd been talking to my mom, who went through another round of jitters. She was fearful that, right at the moment when the team and I had made such a splash, coming out might mess things up for me. "Are you sure you're doing the right thing?" she asked, and mentioned my sponsorship deals. She wanted me to consider all the angles before I made my decision, but I told her it was already made. I'd always felt soccer wasn't the beginning and end of my life, which was something my parents had taught me, and now I knew for sure. Coming out was bigger, more important, and more integral to who I was than anything that happened in sports. I also thought my mom's concerns were misplaced. "People are selfish," I said. "You know what people are thinking about rather than thinking about me? Themselves. No one really cares. And if they do care, whatever, **I** don't care."

The interview was published in July 2012, and

my coming out was presented matter-of-factly. "She'll be traveling to London to represent the United States at the Olympics this year," wrote the journalist Jerry Portwood. "It's a crowning achievement for the 27-year-old. But Rapinoe has decided to pull off another landmark in women's soccer: to come out and publicly discuss her sexuality." I said some things I'd been feeling ever since the World Cup. "I feel like sports in general are still homophobic, in the sense that not a lot of people are out. . . . People want—they **need**—to see that there are people like me playing soccer for the good ol' U.S. of A."

I spoke about the fact that while I'd never been actively hiding, since no journalist had ever asked me about my sexuality, I felt duty bound to spell it out. "For the record: I am gay." My sister chipped in with a quote. "I think it's incredibly brave to use this talent and platform that she's been blessed with in a positive way," said Rachael, "not just on the field, but providing an example of how to treat people off the field as well." Then I told the reporter I'd modeled my bleached-blond pixie cut partly on Tilda Swinton, and that life was too short to take seriously. It was a fun interview.

Nothing happened. In the best possible way, it was a complete nonevent. My sponsors didn't cancel me. I didn't get an angry call from Nike. There was no negative blowback, or, if there was, I didn't see it. Coming out in this way felt like a positive thing in my life and career. It also felt part of a wider movement. Later that year, a judge found in favor of Edith Windsor, ruling that section 3 of the Defense of Marriage Act, defining marriage as exclusively between a man and woman, was unconstitutional, and ordered the IRS to reimburse Windsor, with interest. The decision was upheld by the court of appeals, and as it began making its way up to the Supreme Court, I was proud to have spoken up in some small way. I felt like I was part of something bigger than myself.

The only regret was that with the exception of Lori, who came out shortly after me, no one else on the team came out. They were all very supportive and lots of players tweeted in my favor, but when I talked to the other gay players, they mostly said the same thing: I just want to live my life. I'm not the kind of person who likes to scream about my sexuality from the rooftops. If you come out, you have to be an advocate, which isn't me.

I got it. And I got that if in women's sports being gay wasn't a big deal, then you could live quite comfortably half in the closet. If no one cared, why go through the hassle of formally coming out?

This missed the point. If you're a prominent athlete, coming out isn't for yourself but for others. Until everyone can come out without it being a big deal, nobody gets to "just" live their lives. And the more people who come out, the more we break down the stereotypes of what it is to be gay. I would love it, for example, if an athlete on the level of a LeBron James or a Derek Jeter came out. It would mess with the stereotypes about masculinity and femininity, just as if more women on my team came out, I'd hoped it would show there was more than one way to be gay.

I didn't mind being the "gay player," or one of the few out players on the team. Clearly I like attention and I was comfortable with myself, no matter what. But I couldn't understand why no one else followed suit. I wanted to ask them: What do you want to be the story of your lives? Do you want someone else to tell it for you, or do you want to tell it yourself?

I also started to understand the privilege of coming out as a female athlete. I came out and it was applauded; that's not the universal experience, or, probably, even the norm. For the first time, I began to realize it was about more than being gay, and that there were other factors at play. I was affluent and white, and I had a platform, all of which shaped people's responses to me. And while I didn't yet have the term "intersectionality," at hand, I understood that people without my protections were struggling. We're

supposed to respect people's timetables for coming out, and I try, I really do. But guys, come
on; people are still being beaten up for being gay,
it's illegal in over seventy countries, and it's pun-
ishable by death in at least ten. Can you maybe
hurry things up a bit?

9

THE END OF THE
LEAGUE

You get a free pass when you're a successful athlete and belong to a winning team. If you play and win for the US, you're a hero; you occupy a category that is almost immune to criticism. When I came out, I hadn't braced for a backlash exactly, but I had been prepared for some negative commentary, and when it didn't come, I was pleasantly surprised. I was twenty-seven and politically engaged, while also remaining relatively politically naive. Looking around, I came to a general conclusion: perhaps the world was a better place than I'd imagined.

This was not an eccentric mindset for me to have had in late 2011. Months before I came out publicly, though, I had a lot to learn and another season to play. As a soccer player, I was looking forward to the 2012 London Olympics; as an out gay woman, I was following the run-up to the 2012 presidential election with a keener and more personal interest than any election I'd followed before. I broadened my political reading beyond the campaign for equal marriage and gay rights to other minority interests and progressive causes, on the basis that what helped one probably helped the other. What was Mitt Romney's record on civil rights? (He didn't have one.) How was he on the environment? (Terrible; he campaigned against Obama's Environmental Protection Agency because it was "killing jobs.") How did he plan to help the uninsured? (By pulling Obamacare on day one of his presidency and replacing it with . . . tax breaks.) My dad had started watching Fox News, and when he went off about Obama to me one day on the phone, I was ready. "That's funny," I said, "because you got a lot more in benefits for putting in energy-efficient windows and doing construction jobs for energy-efficient updating with Obama than you would with Romney. And Obamacare—I know it's not perfect—but it's better than anything else on the table." I hadn't become any less annoying since college; I had just become more informed.

The big issue for me was gay marriage, and in spring 2012, six months before the election, President Obama had become the first sitting president to announce his support. (Romney went on

Fox News to affirm that marriage should exist only between a man and a woman.) Obama's support was a huge deal and the tide was turning. Just look at the way the American public had changed its mind on this issue over the years. In 1988, a University of Chicago poll found that 67.6 percent of Americans were opposed to same-sex marriage. In 2006, a Pew survey found that figure had dropped to 51 percent. And in May 2011, a Gallup poll was among the first to show that a majority of Americans supported gay marriage. Consciousness could be changed. Speaking out, coming out, being an out gay figure in public life: all of these actions helped. I thought of all the love and support I'd had when I'd decided to come out, and it seemed to beg an obvious question: If we worked together, what else might we change?

Getting back to the US after the World Cup had brought more immediate challenges. The Women's Professional Soccer league had always been underfunded and badly organized, but that summer it seemed as if many of the league teams were on the brink of collapse. At the end of 2010, the Chicago Red Stars had gotten into financial difficulty and left the WPS, and I had left the Chicago Red Stars. I had signed briefly with a team in Philadelphia, before being bought, just before the World Cup, by a Florida-based team called magicJack, for a hundred-thousand-dollar transfer fee. It was pocket change compared to the men's game (a few years later, Christian Pulisic was bought by Chelsea, the English Premier League side, for $73 million, the most expensive transfer in American soccer history) and none of it came to me, but it was still the highest transfer fee in the history of women's soccer and a rare injection of cash into the ailing league. magicJack was owned by Dan Borislow, a billionaire mired in legal disputes with the WPS and some of his own players, but who had splashed a ton of money on the team, which that season included Abby Wambach, Shannon Boxx, and Hope Solo. After the World Cup, down we all went to Boca Raton.

It was strange to settle into life after the tournament. For several months, we'd been the toast of the nation, flying in chartered planes, appearing on TV, playing in front of millions of people. Now we were back to the reality of life in the league. It was a relief in some ways. The league wasn't perfect, but for those of us on the national team, it was a welcome retreat from the craziness. When you play internationally, you go to training camp, play two games in a row, and boom, you're done. If you're not in the starting lineup, you might not even see that much game time. In the league, you can settle into the season and have the time and space to work on your game.

The downside is tiny crowds and a sense of frustration that gains made by the national team never trickled down to the league. This made sense in some ways. There's a difference between cheering on Team USA during a big international tournament and turning up for an under-promoted Wednesday-night game between two teams you've never heard of. But that didn't entirely explain the disconnect. The average league player earned twenty-five thousand dollars a year, and so many had to quit to find a job long before they were ready to retire. There was inadequate investment in marketing and promotion. And the fortunes of most individual league teams were dependent on the whims of their billionaire owners—not an entirely reliable funding model.

Dan Borislow had bought the team in 2011, relocated it from Washington to Florida, and changed its name from Washington Freedom to magicJack, the name of the phone company he owned. He was an inventor and a horse breeder, exactly the kind of guy who buys himself a sports team, which I don't say to disparage him—the enthusiasm and investment of eccentric billionaires are what keep even the biggest NFL teams afloat. My beef that year, looking at the chaos of the WPS, was that when money was tight, or the league failed to turn a profit, those billionaires were quicker to bail on us than they were when backing men's teams—specifically, the less successful players of men's Major League Soccer. The WPS was home to some of the best soccer players in the world, but we were women, and in the minds of many investors, we represented a financial risk, irrespective of skill.

I didn't play many games for magicJack. I had no roots in the team, and along with the other national team players, saw the league season that year as a stopgap between the World Cup and the Olympics. In July, we played against the Western New York Flash in Rochester, New York, and attracted the biggest crowd ever in attendance for a WPS league game—some fifteen thousand people—but it wasn't a number we ever managed to pull in again. In October, as Borislow's legal problems grew, the WPS took away the team's franchise and magicJack shuttered. A few months after that, the WPS folded.

For those of us on the national team, this was more of a symbolic blow than a practical one. It was depressing that another women's soccer league had failed, but it didn't alter our lives on the national team and there were plenty of other opportunities to play. In the new year, I flew with the national team to Canada to compete in the CONCACAF qualifying tournament for the Olympics, and in the spring we went to Portugal for the Algarve Cup. We won a lot of our games by wide margins, as usual: 13–0 against Guatemala, 14–0 against the Dominican

Republic, 4–0 against Canada, and 5–0 against Denmark. For the first time, however, we sensed a sour edge to victory. With each passing game, our world dominance intensified, and we could no longer ignore how badly we were paid.

Player salaries and conditions on the national team were governed by a collective bargaining agreement that was negotiated every six years and was due to expire at the end of 2012. Since the last agreement, the team had been finalists in the World Cup, won the Olympic gold medal, and never lost the FIFA number-one world ranking. We'd attracted huge amounts of publicity and seen TV audiences soar. And yet for tier 1 national players, the basic salary being offered by the US Soccer Federation was still roughly $70,000 a year, with a bonus structure that bore no relation to that of the men's teams. Male national team players received a minimum bonus per game regardless of outcome; women received payment only if we won, and then only if the team we beat was in the FIFA top ten. In any given year, a top-tier women's national team player would earn 38 percent of the compensation of her equivalent on the men's teams. If the men's and women's teams each played twenty friendlies in a year, the men would earn on average $263,320; the women, $99,000. And so it went on. Heading into the Olympics, we were the number-one women's team in the world. The men, ranked thirty-five in the world, had failed even to qualify.

I had never thought too much about these numbers before. As a young player just getting into the big tournaments, my focus had exclusively been on playing and winning. Now, as senior players including Christie Rampone, Heather Mitts, and Abby explained the situation to us and solicited our opinions before talking to a lawyer, my attention shifted. I was still focused on winning, but for more than one reason now. The quickest way to make our argument to the US Soccer Federation was by winning and winning big, and while the World Cup had brought us unprecedented publicity, this time we couldn't afford to come second. As we headed to London and the 2012 Olympics, I felt a surge of defiance. Bring it on.

10

LONDON 2012

In Europe, the crowds really know what they're doing. In America, if you score a goal, everyone goes wild. In Europe, where soccer is the only sport, more subtle plays and skills raise a cheer. Our first match of the Olympics was against France in Glasgow, and the eighteen thousand people at Hampden Park noisily rewarded Abby, Carli, and Alex for their goals. But they also lost their minds for tough tackles, corner kicks, and every time I grabbed possession from the French deep in their half, the kind of detail that most American crowds miss. We were just as much of a novelty for the Euro fans, too: 4–2 was a pretty average win for us, but from the sound of the crowd, we remembered that lower scores were the norm for most teams.

The World Cup had been a bigger deal for us

than the Olympics in many ways; we hadn't had to share the stage with so many other sports. But the Olympics were the bigger event, with 204 countries and almost 11,000 athletes, and global audiences of up to 3.6 billion. It wasn't just a sports competition, either. If our success after the World Cup had taught me anything, it was that we weren't a team, we were a multimillion-dollar business. And while winning was the only real basis for the brand, once dominant, there were steps we could take to boost our value.

I had always loved hamming it up, going right back to childhood when I'd run around doing Jim Carrey impressions or making CeCé laugh by pretending to talk out of my ass. As a team, we'd thought up a million goal celebrations over the years, not just to please the fans, but for our own amusement. To keep ourselves going, we got into the habit of yukking it up and milking the crowd. I started calling us a traveling circus.

The second game at the Olympics was against Colombia, and I had something planned in the event that I scored. The match was due to take place on July 28, which was Ali Krieger's twenty-eighth birthday. She should have been with us; she'd started in all six matches of the World Cup and had played brilliantly, scoring the final penalty that put us through to the semifinals. A few months before the Olympics, in a game against the Dominican Republic in the qualifying rounds, she'd torn her ACL during a horrible tackle and was out. It was devastating. It's one thing to injure your ACL and another to do it when someone wilds out at you while going for possession and you're due to be a starter at the Olympics. If I could, I wanted to cheer her up.

Thirty-three minutes into the game against Colombia, I took a ball from Alex, who'd just decimated the Colombian defense, and looping it from the edge of the box over the Colombian keeper, I watched it drop to the right side of the net. While my teammates mobbed me, I bent down, took a note I'd tucked into the inside of my shoe, and held it up to the camera. "Happy B-day Kreigy, we liebe you," it said. (It should've said "Kriegy," of course—I spelled her name wrong. "Liebe" referred to the tattoo she had on her arm; it means "love" in German.) Watching at home, she saw it on TV and burst into tears.

We won that match 3–0 after Abby scored a second goal in the seventy-fourth minute, and I sent a through-ball to Carli, who smacked it in three minutes later. After our final Group game against North Korea—which we won a lackluster 1–0, and NBC skipped to broadcast volleyball—we beat New Zealand 2–0 in the quarters, and were through to the semifinals against Canada.

My parents had come to support me, as had my aunt and uncle, Melanie and Brad, and their son, Dylan. Sarah had come, too, although I wasn't able to hang out with her much. One of the infuriating things about playing in a big tournament like the Olympics was that our movements were heavily regulated. For the two weeks of the tournament, there were strict curfews in place and sanctions for breaking the rules.

Some of these curtailments applied to the men's teams, too, but they were generally more stringently applied to the women, and this seemed to me to be connected to money. As a rule, the less you earn, the less respectfully you're treated, and vice versa. Think of those NBA guys earning $20 million a year—no one's telling them they have a curfew; they're going to do whatever the fuck they want. With money comes not only popularity and fame, but also the invitation to behave with a certain amount of gusto that's hard to pull off when you're lower down the food chain. We on the national team were treated better than those league players making forty thousand dollars a year, but we still made peanuts compared to the men's teams, and it kept us relatively meek.

The pay disparity also made it easier for the soccer authorities to control us. We were the best female soccer players in the world, but when we played at the Olympics we were required to have roommates. Why? "For team chemistry," said our coaches, but that was nonsense. You don't have to room with someone to have team spirit. You don't even have to **like** someone to have team chemistry with them. It was a weird power play by the authorities and part of the infantilizing culture that surrounds female athletes, where the coaches have more power than the players.

As usual, my instinct was that the best way to counter this was to keep on winning. The more we won, the more power we had, and the more we could change our environment. We approached the semis against Canada with a certain amount of swagger, turning up at Old Trafford, in Manchester, with our eyes set on the final. The Canadians scored first with a great goal by my old Portland teammate, Christine Sinclair. Early on in the second half, I took a corner kick. It was chaos in the goal mouth, a mess of Canadian defense, and by some extraordinary fluke, the ball skipped past all of them and into the net. It's extremely rare to score a goal directly from a corner, and this was the first time it had been done in the Olympics. We barely had time to celebrate. Sixty-nine minutes in, Christine scored for the Canadians again and we were down 2–1. I equalized with a shot hammered in off my right foot, and from there we started to push harder. When Christine scored her hat trick, Abby answered by slamming it in on a penalty kick, and with two minutes on the clock, we were 3–3. We dominated in extra time, maintaining possession and pushing deep into the Canadian half. In the 122nd minute, just before the final whistle, Heather passed to Alex, who leapt up to head the ball over the goalkeeper. As if in slow motion, we watched it drop to the back of the net.

It was an amazing match. NBC, which had torn itself away from volleyball, called the game "an instant classic." **The New York Times** summarized it as "one of the best games, involving men or women, in memory." The Canadians were pissed at decisions made by the Norwegian ref, chiefly a penalty awarded against their goalkeeper for time wasting, a rule referees never usually enforce. "We feel like we didn't lose, we feel like it was taken from us," said Christine Sinclair, and I understood her pain. We on the national team knew only too well what it felt like to lose in the dying moments of a big game. But we had fought hard and deserved the win. Now, thirteen months after losing to Japan in the final of the World Cup, we would face them at Wembley for the gold medal.

Our experience of the Olympics had been pretty disjointed so far. We had missed the opening ceremony to be in Scotland for our first game, and hadn't been to London and the main Olympic site yet. With two days to go before the final, we traveled down from Manchester to the center of the games, in Stratford, East London.

I'd grown up watching the Olympics and clung to certain idealistic ideas about the Olympic dream—for example, the notion of all the athletes of the world commingling in harmony. This lasted about five minutes after actually experiencing it. Check-in and getting passes for the Olympic Village took forever. Unlike a hotel, where everything is nearby, the site was massively spread out and hugely inconvenient. You had to walk for miles to get from your room to the food hall. It might've been OK if we'd been there for two weeks and had time to settle in and orient ourselves. But we'd just played six games in a row all over the country and were exhausted. All I wanted to do was sleep, which made being stuck in what looked like kids' beds with kids' comforters all the more infuriating. The whole village was a low-budget, prefab city and, coming in after being on the road, it wasn't what we needed. Next Olympics, we vowed, we wouldn't stay in the village.

All of these gripes evaporated, of course, when we walked out in front of eighty thousand people at Wembley. It was the largest crowd I'd ever played in front of before and one of the biggest ever for a women's game. The noise was overwhelming. Carli got us under way with a goal from a low header in the first ten minutes, and for a second it looked as if we might have an easy ride. Then the Japanese pushed back hard, hammering out multiple attempts on goal that, one after the other, Hope Solo punched and deflected away. Toward the end of the first half, Christie Rampone stepped in with a brilliant save after the Japanese got past almost all our lines of defense, followed by Hope launching herself at a ball hit by Yuki Ogimi, the Japanese striker, sending it bouncing off the crossbar. In the second half, I sent a ball to Carli in midfield and she streaked up the field with it, outflanking all but one of the Japanese defenders, who she dodged rightward until she had a clean shot, smacked it squarely toward the left post, and watched, time slowing, as it cannoned to the back of the net. It was 2–0.

We didn't dare get complacent. Nine minutes after Carli's goal, Yuki Ogimi pushed up the field and snuck in a goal, leaving us exposed to the possibility of the worst possible result: a tie at full time and another penalty shootout. The Japanese, seeing how close they were to eliminating our lead, didn't quit. Moments after their goal, a corner kick rocketed toward Hope, who leapt through the bodies in the goal mouth to catch it. With seven minutes on the clock, the Japanese forward Mana Iwabuchi got past Christie Rampone and looked set to take the score to 2–2, until Hope flew leftward and punched it away. It was a brilliant save and Japan's last real chance to

Our house on Oak Meadow Road in Redding, a small town in Northern California. Most of my family continues to live in the area, and I'll always consider Redding home.

May 1986. Me and Rachael, ten months old, on my mom's lap.

April 1987. I think of CeCé as my oldest sister; here Rachael and I are hanging out with CeCé.

January 1988. Rachael and I have always been inseparable. We were barely ever out of each other's sights when we were little kids.

When I was five, I told my mom I wanted to cut my hair short, like my brother, and only wear boys' clothes.

Mom, Rachael, Brian, me, and Dad.

I remember watching the Women's World Cup in 1999, when the US won 5–4 against China. Mia Hamm and Brandi Chastain became household names. I didn't think that could be me.

1992. Rachael and I wanted to play soccer after watching our older brother, Brian, play with a local team. There wasn't a girls' team nearby, so when we were six, we joined the Under-8 boys' team in Palo Cedro.

I joined Elk Grove, a much bigger soccer team, in 1999—right as soccer became incredibly popular, thanks to the FIFA Women's World Cup taking place in the US.

When we were ten, we were invited to try out for the Mavericks' Under-12 boys' team. We got clobbered every game. We played for only one season before my parents decided to set up a girls' team.

The early games I played for the Portland Pilots were thrilling. The entire college campus came to cheer us on.

At fourteen, Rachael and I were scouted by the Olympic Development Program. Up until then, I just felt lucky to have found something I loved and was good at.

In 2006, the US Women's National Team called to invite me onto the national team.

I was the youngest and the least experienced, but playing on the field with the best players in the world felt like being in a different game altogether.

After I injured my ACL, I trained hard through 2007 and the first half of 2008 before playing a single game. But in August 2008, I returned to the Pilots lineup. I felt like I was back.

Going back and forth between a 27,000-seat stadium and a 5,000-seat field caused my head to spin, but the change of pace was always a relief.

In 2009, I accepted a job playing for the Chicago Red Stars, while Rachael took a redshirt year at Portland.

The Pilots had a nineteen-game winning streak that year, and we made it to the NCAA semifinals (before losing to Stanford).

I went platinum blond just before flying to Germany in 2011, for my first-ever World Cup. We lost to Japan in the finals, but there was so much energy and excitement about our team. It was on the flight home from Germany when I decided to come out publicly in **Out** magazine.

After beating Canada 4–3 in the 122nd minute of the semifinals in London. Alex Morgan headed a goal with less than thirty seconds to go in overtime.

Celebrating with Abby Wambach at the 2012 Olympic quarterfinals, where we beat New Zealand 2–0.

My parents came to London to cheer me on. Once we won, I was overwhelmed with happiness as well as gratitude for the sacrifices they made when I was a kid.

Jumping into Alex Morgan's arms, after she headed the ball over the goalkeeper. **The New York Times** called the game "one of the best games, involving men or women, in memory."

The night before leaving for the World Cup in Germany, I bought pink hair dye. If you're going to go all in, you might as well go all the way.

Following our Olympic win, I was honored with an award at the Los Angeles Gay and Lesbian Center's 41st Anniversary Gala. I gave a speech about my experiences as an out gay woman in sports. Winning was one thing, but being recognized for trying to change hearts and minds gave me so much pride.

In March 2019, we filed a lawsuit against the US Soccer Federation, claiming "purposeful gender discrimination."

It's hard to re-create the rush after winning the World Cup. Days later, thousands of people lined the treets of New York City.

During the final match against the Netherlands. It took us thirty-one minutes to even make a shot on goal.

A few days after we won, thousands of people lined the streets of New York City to see us drive by. At City Hall, after thanking my teammates and all the people who had cheered us on from day one, I spoke to the crowd: "We have to love more, hate less, listen more, talk less."

With Sue, at the ESPY Awards.

A few hours after the parade in New York City, we were honored as Best Team at the 2019 ESPY Awards in Los Angeles.

In September 2019, I was named Best FIFA Women's Player of the Year, and flew to Milan for the ceremony. I spoke about how vital it is that we have one another's backs: "If everybody was as outraged about homophobia as the LGBTQ players, if everybody was as outraged about equal pay or the lack of investment in the women's game as women—that would be the most inspiring thing to me."

That October, I was honored as one of Glamour's Women of the Year, and the following month I gave a speech at the ceremony in New York City, in which I thanked Colin Kaepernick. Were it not for him and his bravery, I wouldn't have been standing there at all.

Behind the scenes of the **Sports Illustrated** cover shoot, holding a sledgehammer.

With Gloria Steinem, who is one in a long list of people whose activism has enabled my own.

Sue doesn't gush or fuss or make a big deal out of things, but the fact that she dived headfirst into a relationship with me, during one of the most difficult and complicated times of my life, was an expression of such love, tenderness, and strength. For the first time in my life, I allowed myself to truly melt into someone.

Behind the scenes of a shoot Sue and I did for **InStyle** in September.

My family definitely got caught up in the excitement after the World Cup.

Real change lies within all of us. So, what are you going to do?

change the outcome. The final whistle blew. A few minutes of overtime elapsed. We had done it.

As the noise slammed into us from the bleachers, all I could think was: Oh, **this** is what winning feels like. After the World Cup, we had been so excited and proud to have grown interest in the game that it had been hard sometimes to remember we'd lost. Now, as we ran around the field, mobbing one another with joy and yelling at our fans, that World Cup feeling revealed itself to have been a fraction of the feeling we had now. This was winning and it was completely different.

All the practice, all the travel, all the sacrifices made—not by me; I had just been doing what I loved—by my parents and everyone else who had invested in me over the years had brought us here, to this intense moment of joy. For a moment I was overwhelmed and burst into tears. The energy of the crowd lifted us that day and carried us home on a wave of celebration. For a few weeks, it didn't matter that the old league had collapsed and the new one—the National Women's Soccer League, or the NWSL—hadn't started yet. It was even possible, for a moment, to live with the fact that we were haggling with the federation over the terms of our contract renewal and looked likely to end 2012 without an agreement. Weeks earlier, when our lawyers had first pressed them for more money, we had known we were the best in the world. Now, once again, we had the gold medal to prove it.

Following our success at the Olympics, I was asked to make more public appearances. In October, I went back to the University of Portland for the first time since graduating, to be honored at halftime during a game. I signed a lot of balls and gave a lot of interviews, and as this went on, I started to notice a pattern. At games and public events, kids standing in line for autographs told me not just about their ambitions in soccer or how much they loved the game, but also how, after I came out, they had gotten up the courage to come out, too. In every interview I gave, LGBTQ politics was on the agenda, so that by the end of the year I was talking as much about gay rights as I was about soccer or the Olympics. I told the truth: that coming out was the best decision I had ever made and I thought it had improved my playing. A huge part of being a successful athlete is trusting yourself and your body—knowing when you can and can't come back from injury, and learning to listen to yourself. I couldn't imagine being an effective player if I wasn't completely honest. I play my best when I'm free.

I hoped that by talking about all this I was doing something to normalize being gay and counter the fact that so many athletes remained in the closet. At the Olympics, there had been only two other out athletes on the entire American team—Seimone Augustus, the basketball player, and Lisa Raymond, the tennis player—and out of roughly 10,700 athletes in the entire Summer Games, a total of 21 were out. (Based on statistical probability, the estimated number of gay athletes was probably north of 500.) Nothing fired me up more than thinking about how hard it still was for people to come out, and I wasn't going to stop talking about it until that changed. In November, I was due to receive an award from the Los Angeles Gay and Lesbian Center, to be presented at their 41st anniversary gala, and was told I'd have the opportunity to make a speech. I leapt at the chance.

I had done a lot of one-on-one interviews over the years and spoken at countless press conferences after games, but I hadn't done a ton of formal public speaking. My mom reminded me of the time I'd run for class president in high school, citing a speech I'd given involving a tortured analogy about a hot dog, which in her opinion landed very well, and reissuing the advice she had given me back then: "Just be prepared," she said, and told me to think about how I wanted to connect with people. I wanted to keep it loose, fun, and, above all, completely honest, and I was confident I could deliver a message while still sounding basically like myself. Still, as I waited to go on stage at the hotel in downtown LA, I was nervous.

I swear a lot. My mom doesn't like it, and I'm always trying to cut back, but most of the time it comes out spontaneously and I wasn't sure whether it would be OK to do that on stage. Then Lori Lindsey, my friend and national teammate, got up to introduce me, cussed vibrantly, and I decided it was fine. I thanked the center for its tireless work, the real foot soldiers of the fight against bigotry. I said that being able to go into an event on the scale of the Olympics while being an out gay woman—"being a wide-open book and just saying this is who I am, I'm damn proud of it, and hopefully you are, too"—had been amazing. I talked about the wonderful response I'd gotten, and how I hoped this would encourage other athletes and public figures to come out, too.

Sarah had playing commitments and couldn't be there, but Rachael was, and I thanked her for being my voice of reason. I told the story of how Lori and I had sat next to each other on the flight back from the World Cup and talked about coming out—how she'd told me I needed to do it and she wasn't fucking around. I said the words "when I came out" about a hundred times, and each time felt an echo of the original buzz. The experience of winning a big tournament was one type of joy, and this was another: being recognized for trying to change hearts and minds. It felt like the culmination of everything good that had happened that year.

Before we wrapped up, the organizers played a showreel. David Beckham called me "an attacking player with a great right foot" and said it was a shame it still took courage to come out. Some younger women called me an inspiration and a role model. Most surreally, Tom Hanks popped up to call me a "fine daughter of our great country," praise my hammy dramatics on the pitch, and express a hope that, following my example, others would come out. He summarized the way I went about things—"I'm a lesbian, deal with it, then go out on the field and kick ass"—perfectly.

At Christmas, I made a decision. As a stopgap after the collapse of the league, I had been playing for the Seattle Sounders, a team that belonged to the Women's Premier Soccer League, an amateur division that after the WPS folded had scrambled together an elite team. Seattle was a fun place to live, better than Florida in any case, but with the new women's professional league still in development, the argument for staying wasn't strong. I was feeling more confident than ever, and when Olympique Lyonnais, the most successful women's club in the world, offered me a six-month contract starting in January, and for good

money by the standards of women's soccer—
fourteen thousand dollars a month—I said yes.
My decision wasn't just about the money. I had
traveled a lot with the national team, but we only
ever stayed in one place for a couple of days and
never really got to experience different cultures.
I wanted to explore and branch out, experience
something that, after the rush of playing in Europe during the Olympics, I imagined was going
to be great: living in a country where soccer was
everything.

11

OLYMPIQUE LYONNAIS

I don't think the French ever really knew what to make of me. When I arrived in Lyon in early 2013, I thought it would be a fun sojourn with better soccer than any league team in the US could muster and an easy way to see a bit more of the world. When I left six months later, I was escaping a coach I didn't jell with; teammates who didn't want to hang out; and a period that had been lonely, frustrating, and unsatisfying. I couldn't wait to get back to the States.

Don't get me wrong, Lyon itself was beautiful. It's a stunning city—the third largest in France—in the southwest of the country, bisected by two rivers and full of medieval churches, grand opera houses, and architecture that made me feel I was a long way from Redding, California.

Obviously, what I loved most about Lyon was the fact that it boasted the best women's league side in the world. At the Olympics, a whopping eleven members of the French national team played for Olympique Lyonnais, including Louisa Nécib, Eugénie Le Sommer, and Élodie Thomis, thanks to whose efforts the team had won two consecutive UEFA Champions League titles and six French league championships in a row. I assumed I would fit right in.

Things looked promising at first. I rented a Smart car. I had room for visitors in my two-bedroom apartment, which was underheated, of course—this was Europe—but at least the wi-fi worked. I wasn't the only foreign player on the team; Olympique Lyonnais Féminin boasted four other top international players—two Japanese players, one from Switzerland, and one from Sweden. Every club-level team I'd played in going right back to Portland had had international players, and we always put ourselves out to make them feel welcome. As the foreigner this time round, I couldn't see any reason why my experiences would be different.

The stereotype about the French is that they are arrogant, but that wasn't my expectation. To me, France meant socialism or, at least, social democracy, a more left-leaning interpretation of government than in the US, encompassing universal health care and better welfare provisions.

Because of this, I assumed that as a matter of course French culture and society would be liberal, or at least more liberal than in the US. I also assumed the players themselves would be super chill and laid-back. The French way of playing is much more fluid than ours, and almost languid compared to our style. Clearly I'd have no trouble fitting in.

That first expectation—that France would be achingly liberal—was blown apart immediately on my arrival. The headline in **Le Monde** when I arrived in France was "Gay Icon," as if no gay person had ever achieved prominence before. As far as I could tell, there were no other out lesbian soccer players anywhere in France, an even worse record than in the US. When I turned up a few days later at the training center in Décines-Charpieu, just outside the city, it was to a scene of mutual bafflement. A lot of the French players had assumed all American athletes were giant-size and were amazed to discover how small I was. For my part, the romantic image I'd been nurturing of the French as more liberated than Americans didn't exactly match up to reality. I didn't find my French teammates arrogant. I found them intensely reserved. There was hardly any laughing or joking on the team, partly because Olympique Lyonnais was the number-one women's club in Europe, if not the world, and the players seemed terrified of losing their spots.

It went deeper than that. I was used to making a lot of noise, pushing back against a coach if I disagreed with them, and breaking out of established playing patterns to try something new, even if the end result was a wild shot that went fifty yards over the crossbar. I wasn't afraid of making goofy mistakes and was always the first to laugh at myself, which was definitely not the vibe on the team. I got the feeling that, in France, this kind of "rule-breaking"—particularly by women, toward a male coach—was generally frowned upon. The French players thought I was crazy. I thought they were afraid to step out of line. We didn't get one another at all.

The coach, Patrice Lair, was a highly respected figure in French soccer, but we had a tough time communicating from the get-go. The language barrier was obviously a big part of this. He would mutter asides during practice, and even though I would call on a French player to translate, asking sharply, "What did he say? What's going on?" the effect of not understanding everything was disorienting. I could, however, tell when I was being criticized; and although he spoke highly of me afterward, at the time he was really hard on me, always chirping that I wasn't doing well enough. No one else on the team talked back to him or called him out on what I thought was his bullshit, which probably riled him up even more. At one point, he made me play a match with the B team, which I took to be a kind of public shaming.

I shrugged it off—I'd be going home soon enough—but other things bothered me. There was no homophobia on the team, but I was surprised by how intolerant the town itself seemed. Perhaps it would have been different in a large, international city like Paris. But in Lyon, I didn't see any same-sex couples walking around holding hands and the message seemed to me to be clear: You can't be too gay in public.

Making friends was hard, too. It's not that the local players were hostile, exactly; I felt they were "America curious"—intrigued by us and envious of the fact we lived more freely than they did. The bigger problem, for me, was that they weren't very outgoing or social. Practice was only a couple of hours every day, and afterward everyone just scattered and did their own thing. It was bizarre. At home, whatever team I was playing on, we all made plans with one another and ensured that the international players were included and looked after. Here, there was nothing like that.

Lyon got boring very quickly. I was out all the time, bobbing around the city, going to dinners or the opera house on my own, but there's only so much tourist stuff you can do—only so many weekends you can spend silently looking at medieval architecture. I kept thinking: Are people going out and not inviting me? I was never invited anywhere, but I honestly don't think they were deliberately excluding me. It seemed to me they were broadly unhappy, and unlike the Brits, who love being unhappy, the French just seemed . . . unhappy. It was a lonesome and dispiriting time.

I buried my head in training. We were working our way up the Champions League table, which we had high expectations of winning. And I tried to keep up my activism. In February, a year before the Sochi Winter Olympics were due to take place, gay athletes started speaking out about homophobic legislation in Russia. A bill was making its way through the Russian parliament that outlawed "homosexual propaganda," including same-sex couples holding hands in public or gay charities organizing public events. Gay athletes, including New Zealand speed skater Blake Skjellerup, had started to speak out about it, but the IOC and other athletes had been conspicuously silent. I was furious. When **USA Today** called me for comment, I told them my girlfriend and I had been together at the London Olympics, and that if I had been competing in Russia, we would have been breaking the law. "What year are we in?" I asked. "People are still being arrested for saying it's OK to be gay? What is the IOC or major sponsors doing, if anything?"

It was hard to know what effect any of this had, or what else I could do. Whenever I gave an interview, the gay rights stuff was front and center, and talking about it felt better than doing nothing. But after the thrill of winning the award at the LA Gay and Lesbian Center, I had occasional moments of doubt. It was fantastic that coming out had gone so well for me, because others might be encouraged to follow suit. But the extra attention and praise also gave rise to occasional middle-of-the-night worries that I wasn't doing enough to justify the spotlight.

The season ended in anticlimax. After scoring four goals in fifteen matches, including in the quarterfinals of the Champions League, I traveled with the team to England for the semis against the German team VfL Wolfsburg. It was a disappointing match, both personally—the coach took me off at halftime—and professionally. The game at Stamford Bridge drew a crowd of twenty-one thousand people, the kind of number we could only dream of for most league matches at home, but when you lose, you don't care about that. After a lackluster game, we lost 1–0 and were out of the tournament.

At this point, I could have left Olympique Lyonnais and never returned. But I was annoyed to leave France on such a downer. We had crashed out of the Champions League at the last minute, in an echo of my experiences losing the

World Cup final, and my ambition was fired up. All the downsides of my six months in Lyon were temporarily overturned by my desire to have another crack at the European title. Unwisely, perhaps, I signed on for a second season, starting in September.

At least I would have the summer at home. It was an exciting time to go back. I had missed the launch of the National Women's Soccer League, the replacement for the WPS that we hoped would stick around for good this time, and would fly back to play the second half of the season with my new team, Seattle Reign. There were eight teams in the NWSL, including old teams like the Chicago Red Stars, and new ones like the Reign and Houston Dash, and coming in midseason after my months in France was like a warm hug after an ice bath. Laura Harvey, the Seattle coach, was a former professional player from England who had coached the Arsenal women's side and guided them to the FA Cup title. Instantly we had a great vibe. She's a player's coach, someone who is tough but supportive and, I sensed, would always have my back.

The only downside was our new contracts. We would, as national team players, receive fifty thousand dollars a year for playing in the new league, but there would be no real raise on our national team salaries, and our bonus structure was

still inferior to the men's. The federation's case—
that setting up the new league represented a huge
investment in us—didn't hold water when our
salaries were on ice, but after months of fruitless
negotiation, we had been browbeaten into sub-
mission. Next time we wouldn't be so forgiving.

My new team played well that first season,
clocking six undefeated games in a row before
losing to the Portland Thorns—in front of
3,800 people—in the final game of the season.
That crowd seemed tiny to me after six months
in France; but when journalists asked whether
I thought the new league was sustainable, I
pointed out that while we should be as ambitious
as we could, it was also important to be realistic.
As players, we needed the NWSL to be a viable
training environment for national team players
and a way of growing the game in the US more
locally. The NWSL didn't have to be the English
Premier League.

In September, I flew back to France. The tiny
amount of French I'd accumulated in the first
half of the year had evaporated over the summer, but I was determined to make friends, and
if not with the players, I'd look elsewhere. One
day after a home match, two women came running after me and introduced themselves. They
were Meg and Rach, an American couple living
in the city with their small daughter, and big
soccer fans who had read I was in the city. They

gave me all their contact details and said, let's hang out if you're ever at a loose end. Was I ever. I called them almost immediately, and on that first meeting we hit it off, bonding over how we were all dying of loneliness—Meg spoke French and worked out of the house, so she was fine, but Rach was a stay-at-home mom and feeling totally isolated. The fall suddenly got more fun and we're still friends to this day.

Still, I was out of my element, and it didn't help that the team had stalled on the field. In November, after a good start in the early rounds, we suffered a shocking exit from the Champions League before the quarterfinals, losing to Potsdam 2–1. That's it; we were out, and the only thing keeping me in France—the dream of lifting the European trophy—evaporated. I'm certainly not sticking around for the fucking French league, I thought, and right after Christmas break, I quit and announced I was heading back to the US. This suited both sides—the team management got to cut my salary, and I got to go home. I have never been happier getting on a plane.

Before the start of the new season, I would have to find a house in Seattle, and the original plan, made back in 2013, was that Sarah would join me. She had applied for her green card and we'd talked about moving in together, or at least spending more time together when she wasn't playing in Australia. But in early 2014, I started looking at properties alone. Over the course of three years, we'd spent so much time apart that the idea of moving in together at this point seemed nonsensical. There was no big breakup, and although it was more me who ended it than her, it didn't come as a big shock to Sarah. I was twenty-eight, back home, and suddenly—in a good way this time—alone.

12

THE FIGHT FOR
EQUAL PAY

There was one thing I'd missed out on by being in France, and that was being around for the negotiations over pay. In fact, none of the players had done much in the way of actual in-person negotiating, something we later realized was a mistake. After discussing among ourselves what kind of pay raises we wanted, we had left most of the bargaining to lawyers. This sometimes works for women. Studies have shown that when women ask for a pay raise it plays less favorably than when men do, and it can be beneficial to have an intermediary. But our circumstances were unusual, and we had missed a trick. Every year, the national team did better and better while the players became more publicly known. Celebrity is a powerful commodity and we had failed to deploy it. Next time, we vowed, we would walk into the board-room ourselves.

There was only one big sporting event in early 2014 and that was the Winter Olympics in Sochi, which I watched with more interest than usual. The anger around homophobia in Russia was once again in the news, and although the huge spotlight on the Winter Games probably allowed for more people to come out in that country, we all knew the brief change in attitude wouldn't last. In February, I was asked to write an op-ed for **The Advocate** magazine, and I used Sochi as a springboard to talk more generally about homophobia and attitudes toward gay athletes in the West. I didn't think we had a whole lot to be smug about.

There was something else I'd been wanting to say for a while. One of the absurd statements made about gay people in sports is that when it comes to the locker room, gay athletes—particularly gay male athletes—represent at best an embar-rassment, at worst, a threat. "You hear guys say things like 'Oh, what if he looks at me?'" I wrote. "Quite frankly, everyone looks at everyone else in the locker room, and if you try to say that you've never looked at anyone else's junk in the locker room, you're a liar! It's human nature."

It's the same ridiculous argument used by opponents of gays in the military—that they "undermine" morale—when the real menace in the locker room is the guy staring at everyone else trying to figure out if they're gay. Who's staring at whom in that scenario, and who represents the threat?! Not the gay guy; it's the voyeur making homophobic remarks. The fact is, I wrote, if you can't handle being on the same team as a gay person, "there are going to be a million things you can't handle on the field."

With the exception of my dating life during my first year of college, I had never really dated anyone who wasn't an athlete. Looking back at my twenties, I had barely dated anyone who wasn't a soccer player. That summer of 2014, I turned twenty-nine and finally broke the pattern. For a while, the joke was that I only dated people with variants of the name Sarah—I'm a Sarah-monogamist—but the fact is that Sera Cahoone lived the sort of life I wasn't remotely familiar with. A successful singer-songwriter I met in Seattle, we were instantly fascinated by each other. She knew nothing about training schedules, match replay, or future team lineups, and I knew nothing about writing or performing songs. And although both of us worked, broadly, in the entertainment business, it was refreshing to be with someone who had their own thing going on. Pretty soon, we were hanging out all the time. By the end of the year, we had moved in together.

The World Cup qualifying tournament that year was in the US, which meant that by the standards of the national team, it was a relatively easy fall schedule. The first match, against Trinidad and Tobago, was in Kansas City, and from there we zipped up to Illinois to beat Guatemala 5–0, thrashed Haiti 6–0 in Washington, DC, and after avoiding another upset against Mexico in the semis (we won 3–0), cruised through to the final and a 6–0 victory over Costa Rica in Pennsylvania. It was the seventh time we had won the tournament and it put us in good shape for the World Cup. Our new coach, Jill Ellis, who had been the head coach at UCLA and replaced Tom Sermanni in the spring, was as gung ho to win as we were.

We were always gung ho to win, of course. When you have to fight as hard as we did just to get on the team, that attitude is a foregone conclusion. After the failure of our pay negotiations, however, our desire to lift the World Cup trophy was fiercer than ever. Most of us realized that winning the World Cup in 2015 would make it harder for the federation to deny us equal pay with the men, who had never won a World Cup—the furthest they'd gotten was third place, in 1930. To be the equal of the men's team, not only did we have to be the best in the world, we also had to be the best in the world over and over. This time, the stakes were bigger than the tournament.

It wasn't only the pay raise we were fighting for. Inequities between the men's and women's games were so entrenched that they seriously affected our safety. Toward the end of 2014, we learned that most of our World Cup matches were scheduled to be played in stadiums with artificial turf. We were furious. Turf is dangerous. When you fall on turf, it takes the skin off your arm or leg like a cheese grater. It's harder on your back and your ankles. We understood that playing on natural grass might not be possible all of the time—which wasn't the case, actually, because clearly it is possible—but to play a major, money-spinning tournament like the World Cup on turf was ridiculous; it hadn't been used in a men's World Cup for over eighty years. In October 2014, we filed a lawsuit against FIFA; however, in January, under pressure to focus on training, we dropped the suit. But we made another vow: This World Cup would be the last time we played a major tournament on turf.

In spite of the huge viewing figures generated in 2011, there was not much buzz in the run-up to the World Cup in 2015. There were a few big send-off games, but the sense of promotional inertia from both FIFA and the US Soccer Federation was depressingly familiar. Precedent didn't seem to matter; we were always starting from scratch. To make matters worse, the tournament was in Canada, not a big soccer-playing nation. The saving grace was that we were close to America, so at least all of **our** games sold out. But the overall feeling was one of underpromotion, and though Vancouver, the host city and a hub of excitement, was cool, in every other city you'd have been forgiven for thinking there was no World Cup going on.

Our response to all of this, as usual, was to focus on winning. The World Cup was our first big tournament with Jill as our coach, and while winning the qualifying tournament had been a great introduction to her, that was a regional competition. Part of the coach's job is to manage the feelings of the players, and that means not passing on her anxiety to them. This was the first time we'd seen Jill perform in a super high-stress environment and we didn't know what to expect. As the early rounds of the World Cup got under way, the team got off to a slow start. In our first match, I scored two of the three goals in our 3–1 win against Australia, a great opening followed by two underwhelming games—a 0–0 draw against Sweden, and a 1–0 win against Nigeria. We were underperforming and we knew it. Jill picked up some flack in the press for being too cautious, and whether that was fair, there was clearly a problem. Though the team vibe was good and we meshed well on the field, we weren't playing as well as we should have. As the tournament progressed, the tension mounted.

After our 1–0 win against China in the quarterfinals, we dispatched Germany 2–0 in the semis and set our sights on the final. It was scheduled for July 5 in Vancouver and was against our old rival, Japan, who we'd lost out to in the 2011 World Cup final. It was the kind of drama sports fans dream of, and finally buzz had been generated. Ahead of the game, fifty-five thousand tickets were sold. There was huge pressure on us all. The night before the final, Jill asked to see me.

It's not that I thought Jill didn't rate me exactly. But unlike with Laura Harvey at Seattle Reign, I was never quite sure where I stood with Jill. I didn't need superstar treatment, and I didn't need someone to carte blanche believe in me. But I did need encouragement, and the vibe from Laura had always been supportive. "I believe in you so much," she would say, and "You're a great player." But she would also tell me, "Here are the areas you need to improve" and "I believe you can be so much more." Rather than berating me when I failed, she talked about my errors in terms of growing my game while acknowledging that in the biggest moments of a match, I always, always showed up.

By contrast, I never felt in safe hands with Jill. That night before the World Cup final, when I walked into her room, she had a laptop with some film clips ready to go. For the next few minutes, she played a showreel of negative clips of me, replays of moments in which I'd failed to defend or lapsed in coverage on the back side. It was clear she was just nervous and, of course, I understood that. The US Women's National Team had never failed to progress to at least the semifinals in the World Cup, and for a new coach, the pressure was intense. But by talking to me about her insecurities **about me**, I didn't understand what she hoped to achieve—apart from unnerving me right before the game.

Once the montage was over, she turned to me and asked whether I thought I should be in the starting lineup. "Or should I keep you on the bench and maybe bring you in during the second half?" she wondered. I was completely incredulous. "What?!" I replied. "I'm literally one of the best players in the whole tournament, what are you **talking** about?" No, I told her; you shouldn't start me on the bench. I need to be in the opening lineup.

I left the meeting in a daze. It seemed to me Jill was nervous and was working out those nerves by passing them on to me, without understanding what that could do to a player. I have a solid sense of self, but jeez, that would shake anyone, and that night, it cost me some sleep. It was hard to not be rattled and I was also pissed off. Great, I thought;

the night before the biggest match of my career, you've shown me all these negative things about myself, and now that's all I have in my mind. If you're nervous, I thought, call your wife.

Everything we've achieved politically as a team can be dated to what happened after that World Cup final. Before we played Japan on July 5, 2015, we were politically disorganized, so although we elected player reps to negotiate with US Soccer, we had no clear sense of how to get what we wanted. After the final, when we found ourselves, once again, in the absurd position of being the best in the world while being treated like amateurs, we finally stopped messing around. We couldn't keep going through this cycle of winning with conditions never improving. This time, no matter how much work it took, we were going to change things.

The match itself was dramatic, a high-scoring game of a kind you never get in the final of a huge tournament. We went for broke and the first half was Carli's. Three minutes in, I played a short ball from the corner and Carli smacked it right in, boom! Two minutes later, she scored again, and ten minutes after that, Lauren Cheney made it 3–0 with a beautiful volley. We had never felt so confident on the field. Japan clawed back a goal, but by halftime, after another goal—a ridiculous shot from half field that only Carli would have had the audacity to try—we were up 4–1.

We weren't going to let our guard down now. Ahead by three goals in the second half of the World Cup final is a pretty sweet place to be, but we were also wary of getting too relaxed. After a fifth goal by Tobin Heath, however, it was hard to keep our expectations at bay. Even after a clumsy own goal, bringing the score to 5–2, we knew we were home. The final whistle blew. The stadium exploded. We had won the World Cup after a sixteen-year hiatus, with the highest score ever recorded in a tournament final. And to cap it all, it was my thirtieth birthday.

There is nothing like winning, except winning when you know you're going to put it to good use. When we got back to the States, it was immediately clear that US Soccer was unprepared to take advantage of our win and keep up public interest. We were returning to bad contracts, bad pay, and no structure or foundation to build on our global audience. Winning the World Cup was awesome. But it wasn't enough.

We started to talk about organization. Our Players Association was in disarray, so we began auditing the skills of every member of the team to determine how we could put them to use. The smartest people among us were Christen Press, Becky Sauerbrunn, and Meghan Klingenberg. Christen's great at strategy; Meghan's amazing at the business side; and Becky is incredibly clever, which is why they were our player representatives already. Now, we decided, instead of relying solely on lawyers, these were the people we wanted in the room when it came to negotiating our contracts.

We had other usable skills—chiefly, celebrity. While Christen hated doing media, it came easily to Alex Morgan and me, and we could generate publicity, talk ourselves blue about pay and conditions, and put our platform to good use. Our public profiles, meanwhile, meant we hit heavy in the room with US Soccer. This is how we proceeded, identifying what we needed and then appointing whoever was strongest in that area. When you know yourself and your strengths, there is always something you can do to raise the standard for everyone.

As a team, it was an extraordinary moment—witnessing this collection of women rise up—and it fundamentally changed our dynamic. Prior to 2015, the leadership structure within the team had followed playing hierarchies, so those elected to negotiate with US Soccer were always the best or oldest on the team. Now, by looking at people's skills off the field, we essentially established a business within a business. We developed clear goals and strategies. We put systems in place to handle media interest. Younger players were encouraged to speak up and get involved, and natural leaders—whether or not they were the best on the team—were encouraged to take on those roles. It was a better, more democratic environment in which we gave one another space to be more than just players.

I swung into action, giving interviews and putting the pay issue front and center. Right after the World Cup, I did a Q and A with **The Players' Tribune** and was asked what needed to happen in order for the women's game to get to the next level. "We need more funding," I said. "Listen, it's awesome that people got on board and watched the World Cup. And it's cool that businesses like us, but I hope they put their money where their mouth is. The women's game can make money. It's proven. It's not a handout. It's not 'you should do the right thing.' More than 20 million people watched the final in the US alone. That's real money." Without sexism putting a hand on the scales, the argument made itself.

In the fall, we embarked on a national victory tour, playing friendlies and exhibition matches around the country. In December, we were due to play a match against Trinidad and Tobago in Hawaii—on turf. A few days before the game, during a practice session on the field in Honolulu, I tore my ACL. It actually happened on grass, but because the game itself was to be played on turf, everyone assumed the injury had happened on turf, too, and I was happy to let the misapprehension stand. For once, the federation was embarrassed. The game was canceled and Sunil Gulati, the federation president, apologized to the players for a "series of mistakes" leading up to the game in Hawaii. We all knew the problem went much further than that, and although Gulati didn't say so, we felt confident that the publicity around my injury meant we would never be asked to play on turf again.

I hadn't been injured like this in almost ten years. It was a shock. But those kinds of early lessons don't leave you and it was, I knew, important to give myself time and not rush back on the field. In playing terms, we were in a tight turnaround between the World Cup and the Olympics, but I was pretty logical about the injury and knew not to be reckless. At the end of the season, as I plowed through cycles of rest and rehab, I kept in touch with Becky, Christen, and and our fierce labor lawyer, Mady, about how to press the federation for better pay.

One thing we learned: You can't go into a campaign worrying about whether people will like you. This is a problem for women. We're socialized to fear being disliked. In any encounter, the burden of social ease often falls on us. We're not supposed to make trouble, and it stops us from getting—or even asking for—what we want.

Well, sorry. When a male national team player receives $5,000 for losing a friendly, and a female player receives $1,350 for a **win** (and nothing whatsoever for a loss or a tie); when the women's national team exceeded revenue projections by $16 million in 2015, and the men's team was in the red; when there are disparities going right down to the level of per diems we receive when we travel for the team ($50 a day for the women; $62.50 for the men)—it's not time to make nice. At the end of 2015, we made a decision. Keeping things pleasant, civil, and in-house at the federation hadn't worked. Now we needed outside help. We hired another lawyer. We looked to the Equal Employment Opportunity Commission. We took steps toward filing a formal complaint.

13

RIO

Sera and I hosted Thanksgiving at home in Seattle that year. It was a full house, with a lot of my cousins and friends staying for the long weekend. The day after the holiday, I called my mom in an indignant rage. "God, Mom," I said, "these effing people, they leave their coffee cups everywhere. What's with that? I'm making pot after pot, and they act like they're on vacation."

My mom burst out laughing. "They **are** on vacation!" she said. "**In your house**, and you're the hostess." Growing up, it drove her crazy when I left my stuff all over the house. ("Pick up after yourself, I'm not going to wait on you!" she'd yell.) Now karma had come for me and she thought it was hilarious. Looking after people, it turns out, is completely exhausting, and also something I felt compelled—and secretly loved—to do. "I don't know how it happened," I grumbled to my mom, "but I got your hospitality gene."

Throwing our own Thanksgiving was a sign that I had finally established somewhere beyond my parents' house to call home. In August, a month after the Supreme Court legalized same-sex marriage and a few weeks after the World Cup final, Sera and I had gotten engaged. There was so much to be excited about that summer, but being able to marry the woman I loved was right up there with winning the World Cup. We made a public announcement, posting a photo of us kissing on Instagram and inviting every-one to celebrate with us. It was a hopeful ges-ture, one matched, the following March, when I and four of my teammates—Carli, Becky, Alex, and Hope—put our names to a federal wage dis-crimination complaint with the EEOC. We were backed by the whole team, and judging by the press we received, by most casual observers, too. The numbers were hard to argue with; in spite of making more money, generating more publicity, and winning overwhelmingly more matches than the men's team, we made as little as 40 percent of what they did. In the early part of 2016, it felt as if we were forging ahead.

The only sadness was Brian. A lot had changed since our childhoods. Years earlier, he'd had a moment of reckoning in the prison yard, when he'd realized it was self-defeating for prisoners to be fighting one another when they were all being let down by the system. In the wake of this, he'd become quite liberal, an outspoken critic of racism in prison and a proponent of system reform.

In other ways, however, nothing had changed. He'd watched the World Cup from a prison cell in San Diego, where he was serving eight months on drug charges. A journalist had visited him there and the piece was posted, with my blessing, on the US Soccer Federation website. It painted a vivid portrait of my brother watching my games on the TV from his cell, cheering me on with other men who, for whatever reason, had been ensnared in the system alongside him, and banging on bars when we won. It was a positive piece, and a good exercise in humanization, showing, through the medium of my goofy brother, that drug addicts and offenders aren't some mysterious "other," but brothers, sons, sisters, mothers who came from families no different from yours.

Like a lot of the coverage about Brian, however, it was also sentimental in tone. "I think we've even gotten closer [as adults]," he said of our relationship, but I think we both knew it was more complicated than that. If I played in the Rio Olympics the following summer, I knew Brian would be rooting for me all the way. But while I kept up with his news through my mom and we texted sporadically, the truth is I hadn't seen him in years.

I was still coming back from my knee injury that spring. The recovery process was grueling, full of six-hour days of rehab and training. I knew from experience that my body was healing and that if I could be patient, I'd get to the other side. In the meantime, I tried to focus on other things. That March of 2016, I flew to New York to speak at Cornell University for the launch of Athlete Ally, an LGBTQ advocacy group. "I have walked in your shoes, and walked the road ahead of you, and want you to know you will be OK, and you have more support than you ever dared to dream of," I'd said when I joined the organization, addressing young gay athletes. Now I was excited to talk to students.

Since the first big speech I'd made at the LA Gay and Lesbian Center, I had become much more comfortable speaking in public. A lot of what I said was simple and repetitive: It's not OK to discriminate. During my speech at Cornell, I went further: It's not OK to stay silent when you hear someone else being discriminatory. When I came out, I benefited enormously from the support of straight allies in the sports world. I wanted to make this clear to the kids coming up behind me.

I also wanted to discuss stereotypes. In sports,

homophobia is less extreme for gay women than gay men, but it gets mixed up with sexism and becomes instantly more toxic. Women are expected to look a certain way, and being gay merely changes the stereotype. There's a perception, I said at Cornell, that if you're a gay female athlete, then you'd damn well better "look gay." Which is fine; if women want to have short hair and wear flannel, good for them. "But what if you don't look 'gay'?" I said. One of my hopes was that as more players felt confident to come out, we would broaden the spectrum of what it means to be gay. Not all of us have short hair! Some players with ponytails are gay! Just like being straight, there's no one way to be, look, act, or feel gay, and being made to believe otherwise is incredibly narrowing.

These stereotypes also flush out all sorts of latent prejudice. It's a widely accepted form of homophobia, for example, for people to insist that not all women in sports are gay—as if they are defending straight women from some kind of slur—and for sportswomen to make themselves more "feminine" for fear of being mistaken for gay. A few weeks later, I did a panel with Abby Wambach at Ohio State University, where we discussed pay equity and how the men's team is paid more for losing than we are for winning. I started talking more generally about image. As our team had become more successful and we'd started doing more publicity, we'd all noticed the increase in pressure on us to look a certain way. Everyone remembered the bad old days of David Letterman introducing the 1999 World Cup–winning team on his show as "babe city," but we assumed that kind of talk was part of the dark ages.

It wasn't. Fifteen years later, a lot of female athletes felt pressure to wear makeup when they played, and while this appeased sponsors, the truth is the pressure wasn't entirely external. We might refuse to be crammed into the "babe city" mold, but as the team got more attention, many of us started looking "cuter" and more conventionally feminine—myself included. These standards are baked into our social wiring and however much you disapprove of them, it can be incredibly hard to opt out.

A month before the Olympics, I was invited by **Bleacher Report** to write a letter to my thirteen-year-old self. I jumped at the chance. Lately, I had become uncomfortable with how youth soccer was organized. I loved the game, of course, but winning isn't everything, and looking at kids coming up twenty years behind me, I was worried by how single-track the system had become, with kids pressured to play year-round and commit to a schedule that ruled out anything else. As a kid, when I got the call to play for the Under-17 national team, no one in my life knew what to make of it. Being offered that opportunity was a completely bizarre thing to have happened. I was off doing my own thing, playing soccer as well as other sports and following my interests with no particular plan. Becoming a "star" wasn't something I even knew to aspire to.

Things had changed since then. The kids today were ranked when they were ten years old. They were fully on the grid by the time they were twelve, and if they weren't, they felt as if they'd already failed. This was ridiculous. You can't, by definition, be a failure at twelve, and there is always more than one path to success. You need huge determination to be a professional athlete, but focusing on one sport to the exclusion of all else is counterproductive. You are not a machine. You are a human being, in a world with other human beings, and while soccer is important, life is important, too.

In my letter, I urged my thirteen-year-old self to look beyond my own experience to see if there is anything I could do to help others. "If you are feeling uncomfortable about speaking out about something, instead of doing it for yourself, do it for someone else," I wrote. "Do it for the people, or the cause, that you are standing up for. Sometimes it's just bigger than you. If you carry the strength of other people, it makes it a little less daunting. Putting yourself out there is hard, but it's so worth it. I don't think anyone who has ever spoken out, or stood up or had a brave moment, has regretted it. It's empowering and confidence-building and inspiring. Not only to other people, but to yourself."

There is so much pressure on young athletes these days, it can be easy for them to lose sight of why they are competing. You hear people talk about how they gave up everything and made every conceivable sacrifice to reach their goal, which always makes me think: Where's your passion and joy? This mindset makes winning a matter of life or death. It shouldn't be. It's OK to fail and move on. The most important thing is to hold on to joy.

In July, I turned thirty-one, a week before the roster for the Olympics was announced. I wasn't sure I was going to make the team. I hadn't played a match in nine months, had missed the pre-Olympic friendly against South Africa, and although I was in OK shape and back to training with Seattle Reign, the other players were under instruction to not tackle me. If I made the Olympic team, I'd be coming in off the bench, and there was no way I would be able to play the whole ninety minutes.

Whether I made the lineup or not, that year the US would have a young team with a lot of new faces. Abby Wambach had retired, as had

Shannon Boxx and Lauren Cheney, who had been a strong voice on the team. Christie Rampone was injured. Amy Rodriguez, another forceful, balancing influence, was out on maternity leave and Sydney Leroux was pregnant. New great players were coming up the ranks, including eighteen-year-old Mallory Pugh, twenty-two-year-old Lindsey Horan, and twenty-four-year-old Crystal Dunn. But there's no question there was a leadership vacuum.

With two World Cups and the Olympics under my belt, I was considered a veteran, and coming back I felt a new sense of urgency. Given the youth of the team, we had a chance, I thought, to establish a new, less autocratic environment in which everyone's role was important. A strong coaching voice can set this kind of tone on a team, but in its absence, it fell to the older players. How we behaved on and off the field would shape the team for years to come, and it was important to get it right.

For all our successes, the national team had never won an Olympic gold medal right after a World Cup. There was a good reason for this. When you win a World Cup, you spend six months after the tournament flying around to suck up opportunities and publicity, so by the time the Olympics roll around the following summer, you're completely exhausted. I probably shouldn't have made the team. But when I learned I was on the roster, there's no way I was volunteering to step down. Along with everyone else, I wanted to be part of the record-breaking lineup that finally nailed the world's two biggest tournaments in a single cycle. We were so confident, most of our families booked their flights to Rio for the gold medal match before the games had even started.

The logistics of playing in Brazil were challenging, to say the least. Four years earlier at the London Olympics, the distance between venues had been small. We could be in Glasgow one day and Manchester the next, with a mere forty-five-minute flight in between. In Brazil, we were facing much longer flights between stadiums. After winning our first two games in Belo Horizonte, we took a four-hour flight to our next venue.

I didn't come off the bench during those early games, which were against New Zealand and France. The first appearance I made was in our third game, in a city called Manaus, on the edge of the Amazon. The match was well attended, with thirty thousand people packing the stadium, but we didn't exactly set the field on fire. I played for thirty minutes in the second half, and although we had won enough games to guarantee winning the Group stage by then, finishing with a 2–2 draw was demoralizing.

And Manaus itself was crazy. The humidity was intense. Everything was damp. There were moths the size of your palm. The night before leaving, we dumped all our wet, sweaty gear—cleats, shin guards, gloves—to dry in the hallway outside our rooms, because the rooms themselves were damp. In the morning, they were all gone. By the time we'd flown another three hours to Brasília for the quarterfinal against Sweden, we were tired, sweaty, and in terrible moods.

Our old coach, Pia Sundhage, was in charge of the Swedish national team, which in the history of all our encounters had only beaten us five times. We were ranked number one to their six. They shouldn't have given us any trouble. But in the first half, though we played aggressively as usual, their defensive play stopped us from scoring. In the second half, with the score still 0–0, the Swedes scored in the sixty-first minute, and for a second things looked bleak. Alex equalized seventeen minutes later, but after Carli's goal in overtime was ruled offside, the final whistle blew, and we went to penalties. After playing for twenty-five minutes in the second half, I was back on the bench. All I could do was watch helplessly from the sidelines.

Alex stepped up for the first shot. It was saved by the Swedish goalkeeper, Hedvig Lindahl, and then Sweden scored on their first penalty kick, keeping the score at 1–0. Lindsey Horan rolled her shot in to equalize, then the Swedes did the same: 2–1. Carli took the third penalty and brought us to 2–2. It was unbearable to watch. Sweden's third shot on goal was deflected by Hope, and here we had our opportunity. Our fourth shot from Morgan Brian went in; we were up 3–2— this was it! This was it! But then Sweden equalized. Christen Press stepped up; her ball went flying over the bar. There was one goal between us and disaster. Hope played desperately for time, changing her gloves, trying to psych Sweden out, but it didn't work. Their final penalty shot went in and the game was over. We'd lost 4–3 on penalties, the worst possible exit, and the earliest the US team had ever left the Olympics.

Even if you asked me now why we lost, I would struggle to give you an answer. You could say it was because we were a young team, or because we were exhausted from travel, but those are excuses. Really, I have no idea. "Be honest about how you approach failure," I had written in that letter to my thirteen-year-old self. "Don't just be critical of yourself, because that can be self-serving. Approach it honestly, assess your performance, and assess the areas where you have fallen short. Correct them and move on. Don't dwell on it. Don't hold on to it." This is good advice, but it has a downside. Not dwelling means I'm still unclear on what happened. The net result was that we weren't good enough. At some level, that's all I need to know.

Even in the midst of our misery, I was sure

of one thing, which was that while it was OK
to be mad, to cry, yell, scream, and feel as sorry
for ourselves as we needed to feel, a lot of that
needed to stay private. This was harder for some
than others. Right after our exit, Hope spoke to
the media, accusing Sweden of playing defen-
sively, like "a bunch of cowards," which didn't
go down well. When journalists asked me about
her statement, I said Hope was a sore loser—she
was criticizing Sweden for using the one strategy
that might have beaten us, and to fault them for
succeeding made no sense. We were all seething
with hurt and disappointment. The entire situation was a mess.

The only solution was to try to salvage some
good times out of the bad. Since a lot of people's
families were already in Rio, and our hotel rooms
had been booked and paid for, I decided, along
with Crystal and Ali and some of the others,
to head to the city anyway. Ali's boyfriend was
Brazilian, and he was going to show us around.
I figured I'd never have another chance to go to
the Olympics as a spectator, so why not take the
week to blow it out and just go? I called Sera, who
had been wondering whether to join me, and told
her to come down, we'll have a vacation.

Things hadn't been great between us. Since
getting engaged, the dynamic had shifted. We
had fallen in love because of our differences. Part
of what was so attractive to me about Sera was

that she was a musician and had her own thing going on, and I loved that her life was totally different from mine. Lately, however, we'd been in each other's pockets. I felt she'd leaned too far into my life and had lost sight of her own interests and passions. This was understandable in some ways; since winning the World Cup in 2015, my life was probably taking up more oxygen than before. And I was at fault, too. I needed to be a lot more up-front and honest when I was frustrated. But I also felt she wasn't reading between the lines. We were totally out of balance.

If we hoped Rio might fix us, we were wrong. It was a disaster from the start. Sera headed to Brazil wanting intimate bonding time, when all I wanted was to drown my sorrows and party. She wanted to take walks and go to dinner and discuss our relationship. I wanted to be in a crowd, having fun without thinking about the future.

One night, we were invited to a party on a cruise liner where the US women's national basketball team was staying. Because the boat was technically in international waters, gaining entry involved a whole pain-in-the-ass process with passports. I sometimes wonder what would have happened if I'd given up and bailed; my whole life might have been different.

I had met Sue Bird once before, in LA that spring at a big media day organized by the US

Olympic and Paralympic Committee. She was a star player for the Seattle Storm and a member of the USA Basketball Women's National Team, with three Olympic gold medals to her name. God knows my own team was successful, but the women's national basketball team was, arguably, even more successful than we were. At the Olympic photoshoot that day, I had been sufficiently impressed by Sue to call out a dumb joke to her, then worry it hadn't landed. (It definitely hadn't landed. She was in her team uniform for the shoot, with hair down and full makeup, and as I walked past, I joked, "Are you getting ready for a game?")

My agent, Dan, introduced us, and we chatted about the fact that we both lived in Seattle and yet had never hung out. A few months later, just before the Olympics, we connected again when a number of WNBA players started protesting about police brutality against black Americans. That summer, there had been a series of high-profile cases of young black men being shot and killed by law enforcement, and members of the WNBA team Minnesota Lynx had started wearing black shirts in warm-up games. On the front were the words CHANGE STARTS WITH US. JUSTICE AND ACCOUNTABILITY, and on the back, the names Philando Castile and Alton Sterling—as well as an image of the Dallas Police Department shield, in honor of five officers killed by a sniper the previous week. It was impressive, inclusive, and inspiring.

The protests got little traction. Black women protesting tend to be met with either sanction or silence, and in the case of the Lynx players, the only reason they got any attention is because four off-duty police officers who were providing security at the game walked off the job in disgust. Later, as more WNBA teams joined in the protest, it only hit the media because they were fined.

It is a source of shame to me now that I didn't respond more vigorously to those early protests. I hugely admired their actions and DM'd Sue to say, I think it's awesome and if there's any way my team can help, let us know. But I didn't do more. I credit Colin Kaepernick with so much, but the fact is that the first athletes to protest were the women of the WNBA, and they have never been given their dues.

A month later, in Rio, I ran into Sue at the USA Basketball after-party. Unlike us, her team had won gold—their fourth—and they were celebrating hard. Her high spirits were just what I needed and, along with Sera, my agents, and teammates, we all hung out until the early hours. Sue's friend Diana will say it was obvious there was an attraction between us even then—that she lingered too long at my table that night. Looking back, there was definitely some lingering. We all made plans to meet up in Seattle—me, Sera, Sue, and our mutual friend and agent, Jess Dolan. I had no idea what was going to happen. But I knew I wanted to see her again.

Returning to the US after the Olympic Games was a downer. There was no parade, no victory tour, no celebrations. We had lost, it hurt, and I was as angry and disappointed as the next team member. I also knew this loss wasn't the end of the story. I had played for the national team for almost ten years. We barely, if ever, lost two games in a row. Losing sucked, but wallow in it? I certainly wasn't going to do that.

14

KNEELING

Just before the Olympics, on July 5, a thirty-seven-year-old black man named Alton Sterling had been standing outside a convenience store in Baton Rouge, Louisiana, when police officers, responding to a call of an armed man, pinned him to the ground and shot him at point-blank range. The following day, a thirty-two-year-old black man named Philando Castile had been pulled over by police in Minnesota and shot at point-blank range. Castile's girlfriend and her four-year-old daughter had also been in the car.

A year earlier, Walter Scott, a thirty-year-old black man, had been pulled over in a routine traffic stop in North Charleston, South Carolina, and shot in the back by police while running away. Twenty-eight-year-old Sandra Bland, a black woman, had been pulled over in Texas for a minor traffic violation and taken into custody, where she was found hanging in her cell the following morning. In 2014, Tamir Rice, a twelve-year-old black boy, was shot by a police officer in Ohio while playing with a toy gun. Three months earlier, Michael Brown, a black teenager, was shot and killed by police in Ferguson, Missouri; and a month before that, Eric Garner, a black man, was strangled to death by a police officer using an illegal chokehold on Staten Island, New York. In 2012, Trayvon Martin, a black teenager walking home from the store in Sanford, Florida, was shot to death by George Zimmerman, a neighborhood watch volunteer, who was acquitted by a jury of Martin's murder.

These cases were in the news every day. You would have to be willfully ignorant to not be aware of them. The day after Philando Castile was shot and killed, a man protesting against his death and the deaths of other black men in police custody opened fire on police officers in Dallas, killing five and injuring nine. America felt like a country at war.

I had never spoken about racism publicly before, not because I didn't feel strongly about it, but because it had simply never occurred to me. I don't like to wade into something unless I know what I'm talking about, and I hesitated because racism wasn't "my issue." I couldn't speak about it with the same force of personal experience I brought to LGBTQ politics, pay equity, and sexism, and so I didn't speak about it at all.

But Ferguson changed that. Michael Brown's death two years earlier at the hands of a white police officer sparked a huge outpouring of protest and anger. Reading around the case, I'd been astonished by what I learned. His death was not about a single racist officer. It wasn't even about a racist police department. The roots of Michael Brown's death lay in an entire civic and criminal justice system that had been set up to abuse black people. The police department in Ferguson ran a for-profit system, in which every year the town's populace was issued thousands of fines for minor infractions, including jaywalking and minor driving violations. The figures were staggering. In 2013, in a city of 21,135 people, the municipal court in Ferguson issued 32,975 arrest warrants, the majority of them to black people. When Officer Darren Wilson stopped Michael Brown that day in 2014, it was to tell him to get off the road and walk on the sidewalk, an exchange that ended with the teenager being shot and killed. Michael Brown's death wasn't a glitch in the system. It was the system.

I wanted to read more and turned to someone I knew could help. Jess Dolan had joined my team of agents in 2015, and we had connected instantly. She was my age and grew up in Chico,

California, a small town seventy miles south of Redding—our high school basketball teams had even played each other. After being raised by liberal, schoolteacher parents, Jess had studied at Berkeley, an environment that fueled her political activism. Like me, her political jumping-off point was LGBTQ rights, something with which she had a deep, personal connection. From there, she started to see how gay rights joined up with other social justice campaigns.

With Jess as my mentor, I started to read more widely. In the wake of Ferguson, I read every piece on racial injustice that came out in the press. I read Ta-Nehisi Coates's **We Were Eight Years in Power,** which includes his hugely influential piece about the case for reparations, first published in **The Atlantic**. In hotel rooms after games and on the bus to and from airports, Jess and I talked about the wider implications of what I was reading. There was no one else in my life in soccer—or anywhere, for that matter—who I could level with in these conversations, and I was hungry to discuss and read more.

Slowly, the dots started connecting. There was no point campaigning for one cause without laying it on the line for another. When I came out, the support of the athletic community and the straight world more generally—the media, the sports world, the business world of my sponsors— was huge. Those who are discriminated against shouldn't have to fight alone, and leaving advocacy to the marginalized group itself—the group most at risk of dismissal or reprisal—is, frankly, outrageous. As the summer wore on and Black Lives Matter became more prominent, I felt as if everyone had a duty to join.

Part of that effort lay in education. Thanks to my reading, I was developing a better understanding of the sheer depth of racial discrimination in America. White supremacy is not a redneck bumper sticker or a Confederate flag flying in some old guy's yard in the South. It's not even the KKK or someone using the n-word. White supremacy is the foundation on which our nation is built. Every decision, every law, every piece of legislation that has been passed since the very beginning has operated under the system of white supremacy—putting one race over another to keep power in the hands of a small minority of white men, by ensuring others are classified as "less than."

After slavery ended, and in spite of ongoing segregation, there was a period during which black Americans actually started to thrive. Greenwood, a section of Tulsa, was known as "black Wall Street," where in the absence of white violence, the black community was robust and black businesses prospered. In June 1921, mobs of resentful white residents raided Greenwood, burned it to the ground, and massacred hundreds of black people. Two years later, in Rosewood, Florida—a prosperous black town—history repeated: a white mob invaded the town, razed homes and businesses to the ground, and massacred the townspeople. The fact that the Tulsa and Rosewood massacres are barely taught in schools is not an oversight.

And so it went on. Ten years after Tulsa and Greenwood, the federal government dug people out of the Depression via the New Deal—only they didn't dig everyone out. Omitted from teachings about the New Deal is the fact that many of the mortgages, bailouts, and loans provided by the government systematically excluded people of color. In 1941, black people joined the army and went to war, and when they came home, black service members were excluded from grants covered by the GI Bill. Low-interest loans aren't much use when banks won't lend to black people, just as college tuition isn't much use in Southern colleges that only admit whites. In the 1950s and '60s, as white people started to buy homes and build wealth, the Federal Housing Administration refused to insure mortgages in black neighborhoods, a policy known as "redlining." Meanwhile, the same authority subsidized entire housing developments that were by law only available to white people.

For black Americans, there have never been

gains without backlash. The civil rights era brought about voting rights acts that enfranchised millions of people, so what does the government do? Starts introducing laws that lead to the mass incarceration of black people, so now one in three black men can't vote. After reading everything I could about social and racial injustice, it became clear to me not only how deep the roots of white supremacy went, but also that it was the system from which all other inequalities came. This was a huge light bulb moment: realizing that we're not free until we're all free; that it wasn't a question of protesting against racial injustice **as if** it were my own cause, but doing so because this was also my fight.

In July, members of the WNBA launched their protest. By the end of the month, the hashtag #blacklivesmatter had hit one million mentions. And on August 26, Colin Kaepernick sat down. The quarterback for the San Francisco 49ers refused to stand for the national anthem before a home preseason game, telling the media afterward, "I am not going to stand up to show pride in a flag for a country that oppresses black people and people of color." A week later, after a conversation with Nate Boyer, the former NFL player and Green Beret who suggested that kneeling was more inspiring than sitting, Colin knelt during the anthem and was booed by the fans. Four days after that, the head of the NFL all but accused him of being unpatriotic. When the story blew up, it was obvious to me what I needed to do.

The first action I took was so discreet the only person who saw it was Sue.

To backtrack: after the Olympics, when we all got back to Seattle, Sue and I had met up. It was a group dinner and the vibe was totally platonic, not least because Sera, my fiancée, was there. We discovered that day that Sue and I were due to play in Chicago for our respective teams during the same week in September, and several weeks later I headed to the airport to meet up with my team. At check-in, one of my teammates, who was dating a player on Sue's WNBA team, turned to me and said, "Oh, I'm going to the basketball game tonight and have tick—" Before she could even finish I'd shouted, "I want to go!" I should've known then. Never in a million years would I land from a flight and drive forty-five minutes to see someone else play, and yet I found myself desperate to go. That night, I showed up for Sue's game.

The match was between Seattle Storm, Sue's team, and Chicago Sky, and when the anthem started to play, I remained seated. It was the day after Colin first knelt and I hadn't told anyone I wasn't going to stand up, but I also hadn't **not** told anyone. It wasn't planned. It was a reflex reaction—outrage on Colin's behalf, a desire to show solidarity, and the conviction that what he'd done made total sense. In 2016, young black men aged fifteen to thirty-four were nine times more likely than other Americans to be killed by police. Of all the unarmed people killed by police in 2016, 34 percent were black men (who make up 6 percent of the population). How could any reasonable person believe Colin and other protesters didn't have a point?

I thought no one had noticed. Recently, however, Sue told me that she'd looked up from the court, spotted me sitting, and knew precisely what I was doing. The fact that she noticed, understood, and still had the discretion to not bombard me with questions tells you everything you need to know about what happened next.

After the game, Sue and I met up. I already knew she was funny and thoughtful. And of course I knew she was beautiful. But while I was excited to connect with someone on what felt like a deep level, what I remember most about that night was how calm it was. Sue's from Syosset, New York, and was raised in a happy, liberal household by parents who completely supported her. She's totally chill, powerfully rational, and, unlike me, not remotely impulsive, so while she loves New York, she always says if she could move her entire family and friend group to

Seattle, she would—the Pacific Northwest better suits her personality. We didn't do anything but talk that night—there was no physical overlap with my fiancée back in Seattle, but if I'm honest, there was an emotional one. Before parting, I told Sue I'd be on the road with the team for another week, and when I got home, I'd figure things out with Sera. She was calm about that, too. "All I ask is that you let me know," she said. By the time I saw Sue again, I was single. I was also splashed all over the news.

After kneeling for the first time before the league game in Chicago, I knelt again a few days later in Maryland. Once again, the furor was instantaneous and huge. White people were mad. Whew, were they mad! Conservative commentators in the media immediately started shouting and yelling that kneeling during the anthem disrespected the military. (You want to talk about the military? Military members die every year because they don't have access to health care and the government doesn't adequately fund them. In 2015, it was revealed that hundreds of thousands of veterans had died before their applications to the VA for care were even processed, and racial discrimination has always pervaded veterans' programs. You want to talk about the fucking military?) The owner of the Washington

Spirit, who changed the pregame schedule so the anthem played while we were still in the locker room, later accused me of "hijacking" the game. When I told journalists I was kneeling to draw attention to white supremacy and police brutality, a lot of white people took it incredibly personally. I found this bizarre. It wasn't their fault as individuals that slavery happened, but it was the responsibility of all of us to address it.

I hadn't been expecting anything like this scale of outrage. When I'd campaigned for LGBTQ rights or pay equity, I had always been warmly received. I knew racism was different—just look at what happened to the players in the WNBA who, after staging their T-shirt protest in July, had been fined, individually and as a team, by their league. It was only after a public outcry that the fines were suspended. As Tina Charles, one of the best basketball players in the world, pointed out, wearing breast cancer ribbons to raise awareness was fine; raising awareness of racism—in a league in which 70 percent of the players were black—was not.

There were far fewer black Americans in soccer than basketball, and when I joined Colin's protest, I knew that my whiteness and the whiteness of my sport in general probably offered some degree of immunity. I was also a woman—loud, yes, but small, pale, and, in the eyes of a lot of angry white men, relatively unthreatening. Even something like hair probably came into play; Colin's hair, an Afro, was much bigger than my hair and, along with the rest of him, simply took up more space. To his detractors, Colin was the embodiment of the racist stereotype of the aggressive black male. To my own, I assumed I'd be little more than an irritant.

In the days after kneeling, I realized I had called it wrong. There is a particular kind of baffled outrage reserved by white people for other white people they consider to be "betraying" their race, and that week I felt the full force of it. The criticism kept coming. I was told I was misusing the freedom the US military had fought to give me, which—news flash!—is not how freedom works. Hate mail poured into my agent's office. People called for me to be fired from the team. My social media feeds filled up with abuse.

My mom called. At Jack's, where she worked, the management had taken down a montage of photos of me they'd had up behind the bar, after customers had started complaining. It had been a bit awkward, she said, but she believed in an owner's right to do what he liked with his business, which I reluctantly agreed with. "I get it," she said to me on the phone. "Racism is alive and well, and I totally support what you're saying. But couldn't you have found another vehicle?"

"Mom, there was no other vehicle with this kind of impact," I said. Using a symbol of America to call out America was the whole point. The anthem belonged to those of us protesting, too. Besides which, no matter what shape protests against racism take, they are always met with the accusation that while the principle might be right, the execution is wrong. I just wasn't interested.

My sister Jenny called. She'd had to unfriend a bunch of people after they'd posted bitchy items about me on social media. She, too, thought I'd been too provocative. "You could be setting yourself up for people not to listen anymore," she said. But when people posted abusive messages online, she flew to my defense. "You will not say bad things about my family," she told those who attacked me. "I will cut you out." Jenny is the scariest of us all in some ways. This wasn't an idle threat.

Of everyone in my family, it was Rachael, on holiday in the Alps, who agreed most unequivocally with what I'd done, but she was still pissed I hadn't given her due warning. This was a complaint I heard over and over; that I hadn't thought things through, that I hadn't planned for what might happen after my protest began. I understood my family's concern. But I also thought this criticism was an expression of privilege. For black people, the effects of protesting against police brutality couldn't be mitigated through planning. For millions of Americans, there was no luxury of "choice" around the issue of racism, and if my actions had caused stress among those for whom this wasn't the case, maybe that was no bad thing.

Jill and I had gotten along fine during the Olympics. For those few weeks in Brazil, there had been no question of me starting most games, which had taken the stress out of our relationship. When we got back to the US, I was in the final stages of recovery. All I needed to do was play.

Coaching is a hard job. To be around a team of elite, confident women, you have to be as big and bold as they are, and if you're not, it's blood in the water. Jill, it seemed to me, was all over the place. She would lay out the red carpet for some players, then yank them for no apparent reason. After Ali Krieger was injured in 2015, Jill would try out someone new, let them play for a while, and when they didn't do well—which was almost inevitable, straight off the bat—she'd cut them. It was devastating for those players, and it also pissed off a lot of other people on the team who'd been grinding away for years without getting anywhere.

The first national team game I played after kneeling was a friendly against Thailand in Ohio. Before the game, I had a conversation with

Jill and two media officers—one from the team, one from US Soccer. It was a short, amicable conversation in which they asked the inevitable question—is there any way you can protest without kneeling?—to which I said no. When they said OK, I felt broadly supported.

Once you start protesting, things quickly get complicated. Before the game, I tried to figure out what I was going to do. If I knelt for the American anthem as planned, was I going to stand for the Thai anthem, when Thailand's human rights record was far from perfect? On the other hand, I'm not a citizen of that country and protesting their rights wasn't my responsibility. On the other hand, we're all citizens of the world. And so it went, round and round in my head.

In the end, I stood for the Thai anthem and knelt for my own, and a few days later, US Soccer came out with a statement that might as well have had "Dear Megan" at the top of it. "Representing your country is a privilege and honor for any player or coach that is associated with US Soccer's National Teams," it said. "In front of national and often global audiences, the playing of our national anthem is an opportunity for our Men's and Women's National Team players and coaches to reflect upon the liberties and freedom we all appreciate in this country. As part of the privilege to represent your country, we have an expectation that our players and coaches will stand and honor our flag while the national anthem is played."

We were at the airport on the way to Atlanta for another game when news of the statement pinged on my phone. In a fury, I went to find Jill. "Have you seen this?" I said. "This is bullshit." The whole thing was absurd. Of course I understood the expectation was that we would stand during the anthem. No shit, that's the whole point of not standing. If we weren't **supposed** to stand, kneeling would hardly constitute a protest. And what had been the point of meeting with the federation's media rep if they were going to issue this statement? It was on US Soccer, not Jill—and to be fair she hadn't signed up for any of this—but in that moment I could've used some shared outrage. Instead, later that day, I found myself apologizing to Jill for my intemperance.

It was a scene that would repeat in the following days. When we got to Atlanta for the game against the Netherlands, Jill asked to see me before the game. As a precaution, I asked my team captains, Becky and Carli, to come with me; I had a hunch that whatever was coming wouldn't be good.

Owing to my performance in the game against Thailand, said Jill, I wouldn't be in the starting lineup for the game that night in Atlanta. "That's bullshit," I said. "We just won 9–0." Two days earlier, Jill had told me I would be starting the game, and now all of a sudden I'm not? She dissembled; it wasn't for the reason I might think she was doing it, she told me, and when I pushed back, she changed tack. It had been very difficult; she was getting a lot of judgment about my protest, and given the scale of the fallout, she was worried about safety. (You live in a gated community, I thought, perhaps unkindly. You're fine.) Maybe I should have had more time for her concerns, but she seemed to be missing the whole point of the protest. Later that day, I apologized again. That night at the game, I was brought on in the second half as a sub.

Everything changed after that game in Atlanta. If Jill had been of two minds about playing me, the experience of seeing the crowd turn against me seemed to help her make up her mind. When I ran out onto the field in the second half, the booing from the bleachers was unmistakable. Being hate-watched piled on the pressure in a way that instinctively raised my competitive game. If you want me to lose, I'm going to win even harder; it really doesn't bother me. But my coach, I suspect, was shocked. She seemed totally blindsided. We beat the Netherlands 3–1 that night, and for the next two games—against Switzerland and Romania—I was told to not dress. (When you don't dress for a game, you turn up but you're in the stands; you might as

well be a spectator.) The reason Jill gave was that
I wasn't back to full fitness. A few weeks later, I
attended winter training camp but didn't dress
for the games. In December, when I broke for the
holidays, I hadn't played with the national team
for more than three months.

Ever since the November election, when Rach
and I discovered our dad had voted for Trump,
we had been giving him the silent treatment. (We
suspended it to send him happy birthday texts
on November 14, but neither of us signed off
with kisses or emojis.) It was rough, the longest
we'd ever gone—six weeks—without speaking
to him, and we'd done it from a place of deep
hurt. Heading home for the holidays, we knew
it was going to be tense. On Christmas Eve, over
my mom's famous annual spaghetti buffet, we let
him have it.

"How could you?!" we yelled. "How could you
vote for that heathen when you have gay daughters?!"

My dad started to object. "I love you guys—"
he said.

"OK, well, Pence doesn't!" we snapped back.

What about Trump's racism? we said. What
about his sexism and homophobia? What about
the way he bragged about sexual assault? None of
it landed. My dad didn't love Trump; he hadn't
signed on to the personality cult. But he was definitely part of Trump's base of disgruntled white

voters who had been persuaded they were a vulnerable minority. What about this? he'd counter. What about that? The social security system was too expensive; Obamacare didn't work; he was upset over something to do with trade deals, all opinions that came from Fox News. "I don't trust the other news networks," he said.

I don't give my dad a free pass for any of this. But I do think it's useful to understand where he comes from. He's from a conservative white town that's been hit hard not only by recession, but also by businesses taking their operations overseas, and his views were echoed by a lot of people he knew. Nothing we said—pointing out how well he'd done under Obama's initiatives to make houses more energy efficient, or how Obamacare provided better access to health care than he'd had before—would convince him otherwise. "Trump doesn't fucking care about you!" we yelled. "You're so worried about Democrats and socialism. You could use some fucking socialism!"

It got pretty intense. My mom doesn't like fighting and tried to calm us down, but we were half mad with her, too. She hadn't voted for Trump, but she hadn't voted for Hillary, either. We know what those third-party votes meant, so she **had** basically voted for Trump. At least she hated Fox News. After years of having it on all day, every day, my mom could see the effect it had on my dad, who had become much more curmudgeonly and defeatist.

It was a rough Christmas, as it was for many families after such a divisive election. I love my dad and admire so many wonderful things about him—his kindness, his decency, his generosity, his work ethic. But when it comes to Trump, I can't bite my tongue.

There were other stresses that holiday season. On top of the Trump stuff, my mom was worried about my safety in the wake of kneeling. "What if someone lashes out?" she said, which I found hard to take seriously. There had been threats, including death threats, but they seemed like hot air.

"I'm a white soccer person," I said. "I'm fine. No one's coming for me." To be sure, this was an expression of privilege, but what else could I say? "I'm not going to live my life in fear."

There was something else my mom was worried about. For the last few months, she had been watching the national team lineups with concern. "You're not getting any playing time," she said. "Are you being punished for kneeling?"

I scoffed. "No, Mom," I said. "Seriously, it's not that at all. It's just Jill being indecisive." Privately, however, I was starting to wonder.

———

In January 2017, I attended a national squad training camp and did well, although not amazingly. I hadn't played a lot and needed more practice. In February, right before the annual SheBelieves Cup, Jill called. She wasn't, she said, inviting me to the pretournament training camp, which ruled me out of playing in the competition. I was flabbergasted. "You're not even going to let me come practice?" I said. Her decision made no sense whatsoever.

I tried to argue my case. If the reasoning was that I still wasn't 100 percent fit, the only remedy was to keep playing. I asked if I could at least come to the beginning of camp, and she told me she'd think about it. The next day she called. No, she said; in her opinion, it'd be better if I stayed and trained with my league team in Seattle. Her words hung in the air for a second while I tried to get a hold on my anger.

"Jill," I said slowly. "There's literally no team for me to play with right now. Preseason hasn't started yet." I didn't say: You motherfucker, you are trying to ice me out and I know it. We finished the conversation and I hung up, shocked and fuming. All those missed games at the end of 2016 suddenly took on new meaning. I had no idea what to do.

The irony was that in early March, US Soccer formally ordered players on the national team to stand during the anthem, something I agreed to go along with. This was a hard decision for me. In terms of my place on the team, it felt very much like a make-or-break moment, and I still feel conflicted about the decision I made. If I hadn't gone along with the federation's rule, my soccer career would have likely ended, and along with losing my job, I would have lost my platform. My celebrity, such as it was, wouldn't outlast my being fired.

But let's be honest: I also wanted to keep playing. I wanted to have that financial security, and I wanted to keep speaking out about racism and police brutality, particularly in light of what was happening to Colin. After leaving the 49ers in March, Colin had become a pariah and remained unsigned, despite being one of the best players in the NFL—the 49ers' "most valuable player of the decade," according to **Pro Football Focus**. It was imperative to keep a spotlight not only on the issues raised by his kneeling, but also on what was happening to Colin in the aftermath.

I was disoriented by US Soccer's actions that winter. But while my agents worried this might be the end of my career, I didn't think I was likely to be fired. If I hit the NWSL season running, it would be impossible for the national team to fire me without exposing the federation to potential legal action. And I was right. They didn't fire me. Instead, Jill and US Soccer seemingly made the decision to put me out to pasture. Judging character really wasn't their strong suit.

Jill never said a word about freezing me out. No conversation was had. Later in 2017, after opening up the NWSL season on fire, I slipped back into training as if nothing had happened, and I can't tell you how crazy that made me. It was so dysfunctional, so dishonest, such utter, evasive bullshit, that my interactions with Jill became strained. I had a big chip on my shoulder. I knew what she'd done, and she knew I knew what she'd done, and while in conversation with her I might have been superficially cordial, my vibe said something else: essentially, fuck you.

I don't wallow, and I'm not paralyzed by defeat. But I can't pretend I wasn't shaken by everything that had happened, and by the extent to which I'd misjudged things. I don't mean I hadn't been expecting fallout, although I was taken aback by Jill's actions. I mean that I hadn't thought I was being particularly controversial by joining in the call to draw attention to a series of very obvious injustices. Privately, many of my teammates and fellow athletes agreed with the protest. Police brutality was wrong. Racism was a big problem in the US. A reckoning was overdue.

Their support behind the scenes was great in

some ways. It also, let's not kid ourselves, sucked. When I first knelt on September 4, 2016, I thought other athletes would join. I let myself imagine the impact it might have if all the NFL players got on board, or the biggest stars of basketball, or some of the male stars in the soccer world, where racism had been a problem for decades. OK, they might not have wanted to kneel for the anthem—but I thought they might step forward to say, We're totally down with everything you're saying, let's figure out a way to protest together.

Some athletes did, including Eric Reid, Colin's 49ers teammate, and later on, various players for the Miami Dolphins, the Kansas City Chiefs, the Tennessee Titans, and the New England Patriots. Not a single white player joined them, however, and in 2017, while Colin languished without a team and I headed toward further dire repercussions with Jill, the biggest stars of the sports world remained silent. It was so disappointing.

15

SUE

While my career was at its lowest point, my personal life was flourishing. A week after kneeling in Chicago, I had returned home and broken up with Sera. (Inevitably, within a week, a whole bunch of people had reported back to Sera that they'd seen me out in Seattle with Sue.) Every relationship I'd ever been in had been hampered by travel and the fact that I was never at home. Now, with US Soccer freezing me out, I was home for much longer periods of time. For the first few months of our relationship, Sue and I got to spend a ton of quality time together. It was—almost—romantic.

At the same time, of course, it was deeply bizarre. Starting a new relationship while at the center of a huge media firestorm is the kind of make-or-break situation you don't really plan for. On the upside, we each got a complete crash course in the other's unvarnished self, the seriousness of what was happening plunging us into real intimacy. On the downside, I was stressed, angry, and generally bent out of shape, and I didn't make it easy for Sue.

She was amazing. Every time I flipped out and picked up my cell, either to fire off an ill-advised tweet or make an ill-advised phone call, she pulled me back. "Take a minute," she'd say, "and see if it still seems like a good idea." When I wanted to freak out at Jill, she'd say calmly, "Don't be an asshole. You have to play the game. She's the coach. You don't have to like her and you don't have to like the environment, but don't fuck yourself or your team over just to win an argument." If it hadn't been for Sue, I would probably have dug myself into a much deeper hole.

One of the best parts about being with Sue during those weeks—besides falling madly in love—was that I got to piggyback on her schedule. I'd always been haphazard about training and diet, never sticking to a regular routine. To date, I'd been able to get away with it, but now with my back against the wall, it was time to step up my game. A few years earlier, Sue had completely revamped her training to improve her performance, and when we met, she was physically on fire. You don't get to be one of the best point guards in WNBA history, with two national championships and four Olympic gold medals under your belt, without amazing discipline and training. I needed to do the same thing.

When Sue trained, I trained; what she ate— more vegetables, less sugar and carbs—I ate. I hadn't been eating enough, which had impacted my ability to train and kept me hovering at 70 percent effort and engagement. Sue's fitness and nutrition schedules not only gave me a sense of strength and stability that helped me power up to 100 percent; they also made Sue and I feel as if we were in this together. At the beginning of the 2017 season, after six months on the new regimen, I was so fit and healthy my entire physique had changed. One look at me and it was blatantly obvious: I was stronger and leaner than before.

I was mentally fit, too. By helping me with my diet and training, Sue wasn't just giving me practical support. It was emotional, too, and during those weeks and months, I felt as if she were wrapping me up and taking care of me, nursing me back to health both physically and mentally. Sue doesn't gush, or fuss, or make a big deal out of things, but the fact that she dived headfirst into this absolute dumpster fire of my life was an expression of such love, and tenderness, and strength all in one, that for the first time in my life, I allowed myself truly to melt into someone.

And we had fun. Sue is super witty and

occasionally I'm funny, too—but wow, she made me work for the laughs. Sue's a tough crowd, allergic to fake laughter (which I'll settle for), so when I made a joke, 90 percent of the time she'd find it funny enough. One in ten times, however, she'd really—**really**—laugh at my joke, and to bank one of those was the best feeling in the world.

During those early months together, Sue was out to her friends, teammates, and family, but she wasn't publicly out. "Hey," said my sister sarcastically a few weeks after Sue and I started dating. "When is Sue coming out? 'Cause, you know; you're the outtest person in the world and . . . kind of visible right now." Sue is more private than I am, and had never felt the need to make a public announcement. But when it was clear we were firmly together, she scheduled an interview with ESPN.

For the first time, I felt something I wasn't accustomed to feeling: vulnerable. I had been in love before, but at thirty-one, I'd never really had my heart broken. My relationship with Sue felt different. On the one hand, it had the ease and inevitability of something that feels truly right. On the other, while I was fully confident of my relationship, falling that hard for someone was new to me. I was more myself with Sue than with anyone I'd ever been with, but I also needed to be my best self—so as not to lose her. I tell her this to this day: If she ever breaks up with me, I'll crumble to dust.

In the spring of 2017, the women's national team and US Soccer negotiated a new collective-bargaining agreement. Our complaint to the EEOC was still working its way through the system, and we were frustrated. Over long meetings in the boardroom, our player reps asked the federation for a new profit-sharing model to reflect the huge gains in revenue generated by the success of the women's team. (They said no.) We negotiated our bonuses up by a few thousand dollars per game, but they were still lower than the men's rates. (We'd asked for the same deal as the men, but the federation rejected it.) For Becky Sauerbrunn, Christen Press, and Meghan Klingenberg, trying to make a deal with the federation while meeting training camp commitments was difficult, and we all got the feeling US Soccer was using our dedication to the sport against us. When we settled on a less-than-perfect deal, it was partly as a matter of expediency; it was clear US Soccer wasn't willing to give us more, and the team wasn't in a place—politically or emotionally—where we were ready to strike. We hadn't come close to achieving equal pay, but we had to get back to the game.

Or at least some of us did. While I was still

in the deep freeze, working out with Sue in Seattle, the national team was playing its spring schedule. It had a bumpy start. In March, the team lost two friendlies back-to-back, to England and France. In April, we beat Russia twice in a pair of friendlies, during which I was permitted to make a very brief appearance toward the end of each game. I hadn't played a full match for the national team since September 2016, and in June, in a game against Sweden, I came on, once again, in the last minutes, before being benched for the next game against Norway. Meanwhile, I was at training camps but wasn't getting any playing time. I wasn't out of the woods yet.

For the first four months of 2017, I trained like a maniac, and when I came back I was in the best shape I'd ever been. I had never worked so hard or been so galvanized, and when the league season started again, I crushed it. Laura, my coach at Seattle Reign, had backed me to the hilt over kneeling. Now she encouraged me to get back in the game, and I was one of the top goal scorers that season. Even Jill couldn't ignore it.

In July, we were due to play in the inaugural Tournament of Nations, a newly established set of friendlies scheduled to take place over the course of a week across the US. After three months of dominating my league games, Jill pretty much had to put me in a starting lineup. The game was in Seattle, and after so many months out of action, I shot out onto the field like a cannon. It can take a while to get into your stride, however, and after a choppy few weeks the whole team was off balance. Australia was ranked seventh to our first, but we ended up losing 1–0, a terrible result by our standards.

A few days later, we played Brazil in San Diego, and it looked as if this game would go the same way. With twelve minutes on the clock, we found ourselves 3–1 down. I was starting to find my rhythm again, and slipped the ball to Christen Press, who flicked it into the net with a business-like touch. A minute later, she made the perfect pass to me on the left side of the box and I smashed it into the near side of the goal. A few minutes after that, I passed to Kelley O'Hara from the right flank, who landed the cross to Julie Ertz, and—boom!—we were up! Moments later, the whistle blew on our last-minute 4–3 win. I was back, and four days later, when we met Japan in Carson, California, I was playing well straight off the bat. Twelve minutes into the game, I wrong-footed Aya Sameshima before coolly slotting the ball into the far post. We won 3–0.

The Tournament of Nations didn't receive a ton of publicity, and most of the games were attended by fewer than twenty thousand fans. But losing still stung. After our defeat against

Australia, we ended up coming second in the tournament, which brought a lot of the team's unhappiness to the fore. Jill wasn't popular, particularly for the way she made decisions, and now we were having a poor season. At the end of July, a group of players complained to the federation on behalf of the team and asked them to find us a new coach.

I don't think we really expected them to fire her. Power is where the money is, and elite female athletes are serially underpaid. If a star male athlete hates his coach, **he's** not going anywhere. The same couldn't be said for us. On the other hand, we did hope that by raising our concerns about Jill's management style, the federation might hear us out and do something to help. Instead, to our amazement, the bosses at US Soccer sat on the complaint for months, and when we pushed back, they obliquely threatened the team, noting that the only person guaranteed to be going to France for the World Cup in 2019 was Jill.

Putting our dissatisfaction on the record still felt good. By bringing everything out into the open, it made many of us on the team realize we weren't the only ones feeling dissatisfied with Jill. Bonding among players improved, morale went up, and as a consequence the team played even better—successes that Jill herself reaped. We were still at the ultimate mercy of the coach and

US Soccer, but mentally, something had shifted. By talking, organizing, and keeping one another in the loop, we were able to present a collective front that, psychologically at least, changed the balance of power. From then on, we controlled the team.

Speaking up can be its own reward, too, and in July, in different circumstances, Sue enjoyed a similar experience. In her interview with ESPN, she formally came out and confirmed we were a couple. Years earlier, I had discovered the difference between coming out privately and publicly, and now I watched Sue go through the same process. To straight observers, coming out publicly might seem like no big deal given she'd never tried to hide in the first place, but believe me, when you belong to a minority that still comes under attack, there is something incredibly freeing about speaking out in public.

In subtle and not-so-subtle ways, I tried to encourage this mindset in my teammates. Coming out, like deciding to protest, is a very private decision and no one should ever be browbeaten into doing it. But it seemed to me, that summer, that standing up against fear and intimidation was more important than ever before. In August, a group of white supremacists, emboldened by Trump's rhetoric, held a rally in Charlottesville, Virginia, in which they marched around carrying tiki torches and flying Confederate and neo-Nazi flags. When violence broke out and a counterprotester was killed, the president made a statement in which he said there were "very fine people on both sides." His words were a green light for white nationalists everywhere.

In August, Malcolm Jenkins, an African American player for the Philadelphia Eagles, raised a fist during the anthem of a preseason game. His teammate Chris Long, a white player who grew up in Charlottesville, put an arm around him. "I think it's a good time for people that look like me to be there for people that are fighting for equality," said Long.

A few weeks later, Aaron Rodgers, quarterback for the Green Bay Packers, knelt during a game warm-up and posted a photo of it on Twitter, which Tom Brady—quarterback for the New England Patriots, and one of the biggest white stars of the NFL—"liked." It wasn't exactly momentous. But it was better than nothing.

The overwhelming majority of those speaking up continued to be black players. In September, when Michael Bennett of the Seattle Seahawks and Marshawn Lynch of the Oakland Raiders staged anthem protests before games, Bennett told CNN that "Charlottesville was the tipping point for me," and said that more white players needed to join. It was an expression of the very racism he was trying to expose that, as Bennett said, "It would take a white player to really get things changed." The corresponding silence from white players was deafening.

There were moments that fall when I worried nothing on any front would ever change for the better. In October, FIFA announced its short list for the Best FIFA Women's Player award. Along with Lieke Martens of the Netherlands and our own Carli Lloyd, one of the players on the short list was someone none of us had heard of and who had never even played professionally—an amateur player for Florida State. Meanwhile, the Australian player Samantha Kerr, who'd arguably had the best year of any player in the world, wasn't even on the list. It was pretty depressing that the highest soccer authority in the world couldn't even identify the sport's best players, and I was furious. FIFA, I told journalists, was "old, male, and stale." Clearly the organization couldn't care less about the women's game.

Toward the end of 2017, Jill sent me an email. She wanted to schedule a meeting, she said, and Dan Flynn would be there. Dan Flynn: CEO of the federation, who only ever turned up to a meeting when someone was about to get fired. "Just curious," I replied casually, "what's the purpose of the meeting?"

"Expectations," wrote Jill, and I went ahead

and freaked out. There was no way I was going
to the meeting alone. I wanted witnesses, and
after calling Becky and Carli, the team captains,
I wrote back to inform Jill I'd be coming to the
meeting, and two of my teammates would be
with me.

As it turned out, Jill didn't want witnesses. She
messaged me to say she thought it would be better if it was just the two of us, and we ended up
downsizing to an informal meeting. She said my
behavior that year had been questionable, not a
reference to kneeling, but to my conduct since
being let in from the cold. My attitude during
training was "toxic," she said, and told me other
players had complained. I didn't believe this. I'm
not a bad teammate, and I hadn't given anyone
else the attitude I'd given Jill. But this conversation was her way of telling me to back off, and
I heard her. We still had to work together. I
backed off.

If I toed the line during practice, I continued
to speak out off the field. By the end of 2017,
something had become very obvious: If you elect
a president on the basis of his attacks on one group
of people, it ends up being bad for us all. I don't
know if everyone understood at the time that
when Trump denigrated women, immigrants,
or the differently abled on the campaign trail, it
wasn't just "a joke." Those words mattered. To
those people who said we'll see how he does in

office, fine. But we—black people, gay people, people with disabilities, the vulnerable—all of us fucking knew what was going to happen.

Once again, I started to think more seriously about how everything joined up. You can't defend gay people without understanding the threat posed to black people and other people of color by their enemies. And look at a concern like housing. Housing insecurity among young people is the junction at which a variety of other issues meet—sexual abuse, drug addiction, domestic violence, mental illness, as well as LGBTQ and racial inequality. Often these kids are abandoned with nowhere to turn but the streets, an unacceptable reality in the world's richest country, but also a wake-up call about "them" and "us." We're all part of the same story. It all connects. When you pick an issue you care about and speak up, you help a range of causes you may know nothing about. When levels of inequality fall for one group, we all rise a little higher across the spectrum.

There are hard and soft protests. In spring 2018, with what I hoped was my worst year behind me, Sue and I did something giddy and hopeful. We had agreed to be the first gay couple to appear in **ESPN the Magazine's** "Body Issue," and now we agreed to pose naked for the cover. It was silly in some ways, a huge glossy shoot for a celebrity product that doubled as an exercise in personal branding. In spite of that, the shoot still felt meaningful: to be the first, to be out, to be proud.

We shot in Seattle. We were both used to being naked in the locker room with strangers wandering around—trainers, coaches, doctors—and neither of us was particularly self-conscious. (Some players turn their backs when they change, but it takes a lot of work to be that modest, and that wasn't us.) We felt very comfortable with Radka Leitmeritz, the female photographer, and since we're competitive, we got into the spirit of wanting to get the best shot without the process taking a thousand hours. The final result, in which we were shown leaping in poses that showed off all the hard work of training, was stunning. But there were shots of us touching each other lovingly, too—Sue's hand on my shoulder, my hand on her arm—which were in some ways a much bigger deal. The whole thing was a big, splashy way of normalizing gay relationships.

Afterward, we spoke to Jemele Hill, a reporter for ESPN. She asked us how it felt to be symbols to a lot of people, and Sue talked about coming out earlier in the year. "'Cause everybody in my life knows. It was not a surprise or shock," she said. "But that's not the same as coming out. It really isn't. Being around Megan, I learned that. And then after I came out, just seeing the reactions, having people come up to mc directly—" I was naturally outspoken; Sue was naturally reserved—but coming out publicly had struck us in exactly the same way, as a vital form of visibility. "I think there's just something really powerful about that."

16

DESERVING

I made about five hundred thousand dollars in 2018. Unless you earn millions and want everyone to know, talking about how much you make is taboo—which has never made sense to me. Without transparency, how do you even know you have a bad deal, or by what metric your work is being judged? If everyone talked about how much they made, discrepancies would be harder to hide. I'd rather know, and tell. Otherwise, trying to estimate what your work is worth is just taking a shot in the dark.

For example: I think many often assume that a Nike sponsorship deal for an athlete like me is worth hundreds of thousands. In fact, my Nike contract was a four-year deal negotiated in 2016, right after I'd injured my ACL, and was worth around eighty thousand dollars a year. As far as

I know, even those of my teammates who struck sponsorship deals at the tops of their games never made far into the hundreds of thousands. This is a nebulous part of the pay equity problem: Female athletes, in my experience, are paid for what we've already done, while men are paid for what they could do in the future. We have to prove ourselves; they only have to show promise. And then when we outperform expectation, we're asked, "Well, are you going to do it again?" We're always playing catch-up.

In the spring of 2018, with our EEOC filing still lumbering along, the team started talking about world championship prize money. We were a year out from the 2019 World Cup in France and in the best shape of our lives. From our first match in January to our final match in November—a 5–1 win against Denmark and a 1–0 win against Scotland, respectively—the US National Women's Team didn't lose a single game in 2018. It was a very good year for me personally. During a friendly against Mexico in April, I scored a goal and broke my own match record with four assists in a single game, taking the final score to 6–2. Over the course of the year, my goal and assist tally would rise to nineteen, the best annual performance of my career.

To ask for more prize money in these circumstances did not seem unusual. In 2015, when we won the World Cup in Canada, the team had received $2 million out of an overall pool of $15 million in prize money. By contrast, the prize pool for the forthcoming 2018 men's FIFA World Cup in Russia was set at $400 million. The men's World Cup enjoys more revenue and higher viewing figures than the women's, but not by a margin that justifies the numbers. According to FIFA's own records, the 2015 Women's World Cup final was watched by a global audience of 850 million viewers, of whom 25 million were in the US, making it the most-watched soccer match ever broadcast in North America. The men's final in 2018 would be watched by a global audience of 1.1 billion, only 14 million of whom were in the US. While there was an argument that the men's game couldn't get any bigger, the women's game was clearly a vast reservoir of untapped growth.

Part of the problem for women is that when it comes to asking for raises, we've been socialized to not make "selfish" demands. We can advocate for our families, or in the service of a cause or campaign, but if we're simply asking for more money on our own behalf and because we have the temerity to believe we deserve it, we are liable to be called greedy. And the problem doesn't end when we have the money; we are also supposed to feel bad about spending it.

I have never felt guilty about splurging. Sue's closet is 75 percent sneakers—that's her big spend—but I love it all: bags, shoes, clothing, moisturizers, jewelry, the whole nine yards. I have a Celine loafer habit. I love my tech (iPad, Mac-Book, AirPods for travel). Since my earliest days playing for the Red Stars, when I flew CeCé out to Chicago for her fortieth birthday, I've always liked spending money on my family. I'm sensible with money to the extent that I invest in property and consult with my uncle Brad, who's my financial adviser, before doing anything too wild, but I think it's OK to enjoy what I earn. And if women are considered "selfish" for doing so? No, thanks; I'm opting out of that.

I'm also opting out of mandatory gratitude. In October, after we'd cruised through the CONCACAF World Cup qualifying rounds, winning the tournament for the eighth time in nine years, FIFA announced that the prize pool for the 2019 Women's World Cup would be doubled to $30 million. It was an entirely random figure, with no rhyme or reason behind it. What was the metric? How did they get to $30 million? By using the magic phrase "doubling the money," they seemed to think they'd so dazzle and overwhelm us that we wouldn't notice there was still a $370 million shortfall with the men. "I think they're probably looking for pats on the back for the increase," I told journalists. "They're not getting any from here. Fifteen million is nothing to them."

If they wanted to come up with an arbitrary figure, I suggested, they could go with a clean $100 million.

At the end of the year, I went home for the holidays and Sue accompanied me for some of the time. My family loves Sue. They can see how good she is for me, how easy we are together, and how she irons out so many of my shortcomings—I can only hope I do the same for her. I can be pretty absentminded; my sister Jenny has never let me live down the time we'd done a Secret Santa and I'd forgotten to buy her a gift. ("That would never happen with Rachael or CeCé," Jenny was still saying years later. "The only person that would happen with would be Megan." Totally true and I'm still mortified.) Now everyone in my family can bypass me and go straight to Sue, who never forgets anything.

My hometown was in a downbeat mood that December. In late July, a terrible fire had broken out, set off by a spark from a vehicle. When my mom called to tell me, I had been in Kansas City for a game against Japan. My mom calls with local news all the time, but this was different. After we'd spoken, I looked up the fire on the internet and couldn't believe what I was seeing. The mountains I'd gazed on thousands of times growing up were engulfed in solid sheets of flame.

It looked like a scene from hell. After burning for a few days in the hills, the fire had spread to the town's residential areas, and thirty-eight thousand people had been evacuated from downtown Redding. My family was safe, but over the next few weeks, the blaze would kill eight people and destroy over a thousand homes.

I immediately put together a Facebook fundraising page. People had lost everything, escaping their homes with just the clothes on their backs. I was devastated watching my hometown suffer like this, and within two weeks of launching the page, thanks in part to the generosity of my teammates, we had raised about $150,000. I had zero time for people bringing up politics in this moment, and when someone posted a message saying they wouldn't donate because I'd disrespected their flag, I lost it.

"First of all, the flag is OUR flag, NOT your flag," I wrote. "Second, there are plenty of people in Redding who wholly disagree with my choice to kneel, donate to THEM and their families. People who had 20 mins to grab their whole life out of their homes. Deal??" The idea that disagreeing with someone disqualifies them from care is absurd. Watching footage of the fire, the only reasonable response was to reach for your wallet and say, "How can I help?"

We had an unusually conflict-free Christmas. The previous year, my sister and I had again spent the entire holiday haranguing my dad about Fox News and Trump. Now we avoided the topic. None of us had the heart to fight, and when I returned to training camp in January, it was with a renewed sense of mission I often felt after spending time with my family. Who I am isn't tied to winning or losing, but to the people who love me no matter what.

I understood, in early 2019, that the EEOC, like so many other agencies, was at risk of having its budgets slashed by Trump and probably wouldn't deliver the outcome we needed. Sure enough, in February, our lawyer received a letter from the agency saying they had failed to reach a decision, and for further redress, we had a "right to sue" in federal court. On March 8, we filed a lawsuit against the United States Soccer Federation, claiming "purposeful gender discrimination." This was a clear-cut case, we said, of women being paid and valued less for our work because of our gender. By launching the suit, we hoped to not only achieve equality for our team, but also to advocate for women athletes around the world.

After news of the lawsuit came out, there was a lot of chatter about timing. Would we be fatally distracted heading into the World Cup in June? Would it interfere with our training? All the responsibility for the suit was put on us rather than on the federation for forcing us into this position, but I can't say we felt particularly rattled. For what seemed like the umpteenth time, we found ourselves approaching a major tournament with a pay dispute hanging over our heads, and if the math didn't make sense—that in order to be paid equally with a men's team that a year earlier had failed to even qualify for the World Cup, we would have to win the fucking thing—we were used to it. We welcomed the extra pressure.

Regardless of how many World Cups you play, you never get used to the buzz, and there is no World Cup buzz quite like the one generated by France. We knew the crowds would be spectacular, and on a whim, the night before leaving, I bought some pink hair dye. Eight years earlier, I'd gone platinum just before flying to Germany for my first-ever World Cup, which hadn't gone down well with everyone. "It's so stark—what have you done?" said my mom, peering at me critically over FaceTime. Now, as I held the pink hair dye in hand, Sue looked at me doubtfully.

"Is this really what you want to do the day before you're going to be on the biggest stage of your life?" she said. I thought for a minute. "That's exactly why I want to do it!" I said. When you're about to be in the trenches, it's a good idea to lighten up, and pink hair is definitely one way to do it. "Oh my gosh, it looks like cotton candy," said my mom, in a replay of 2011. She'd gotten used to the platinum eventually, however, and I was pretty confident she'd come around to the pink. If you're going to go in, you might as well go in all the way.

We landed in France in the first week of June to a degree of excitement I'd never experienced. Eight years earlier, at the World Cup in Germany, women's soccer had hardly been on the map, while four years earlier, in Canada, the World Cup had been flat until the final stages of the tournament. From the get-go, in France, it felt like the entire nation was watching.

At home, our fans watch a match as they might a movie, enjoying what happens on the field more or less passively. The French, on the other hand, know every nuance of the game and, like the English, have all the songs and chants ready. From our first match in Reims, against Thailand, the atmosphere was amazing. Thanks to Alex Morgan's five goals, and goals by a host of World Cup newbies, we won an astonishing 13–0, a score so lopsided we were accused by some journalists of being unsportsmanlike for celebrating. As we made our way through the Group stage, traveling between stadiums in Paris and Le Havre and beating Sweden and Chile along the way, we didn't let in a single goal. By the time we reached the final rounds, we had our eyes firmly placed on the championship title.

———

We beat Spain 2–1 in the round of sixteen—I'd scored both goals, both from penalty kicks—and we were looking forward to a luxurious three days off before meeting France in the quarterfinals. The next day, Dan, my agent, called me with a heads-up. An interview I'd given in January to the soccer magazine **Eight by Eight** had finally hit the newsstands, and with it, a behind-the-scenes video made during the cover shoot. In an off-the-cuff moment, I'd been asked whether I was excited about going to the White House if we won the World Cup. Without thinking, I'd muttered, "I'm not going to the fucking White House." I doubted we'd even be invited, I said. That was it, the extent of the exchange. But it was enough.

The reaction was immediate and massive. Within a day, 12.5 million people had watched the clip on Twitter. Angry commentary started pouring across social media, and right-wing TV hosts picked up my statement as a talking point. The response was intense, like a long-range aftershock from kneeling, but it might well have ended there had it not been for the extraordinary reaction from the White House. The president of the United States of America, apparently with nothing better to do, tweeted out a response to the video, simultaneously inviting the team to the White House and accusing me of having disrespected the country by kneeling.

His tweet was hilariously confused, an indication of just how confounded Trump was by us, and by me personally. On the one hand, we were everything he loves—WINNERS, athletes, people who represent America. On the other, we were women, many of us lesbians, who openly criticized him. In one mad tweet, he'd collapsed under the weight of his own contradictions, and it was a spectacular thing to watch. I hadn't gone into the World Cup proposing to make it political; but on Trump's invitation, I was more than happy to oblige.

I couldn't get fully into it that week; I had to focus on the game. But the night before the quarterfinals, at a scheduled press conference, I made a short statement standing by my remarks, apologizing for swearing (which my mom, among others, hadn't liked), and adding that I was urging my teammates to boycott the White House, too. They didn't need much encouragement. A month earlier, Alex Morgan had told **Time** magazine she wouldn't go to the White House if we won, and now Ali Krieger and other teammates tweeted in support. To her credit, Jill publicly backed me, and the comments went down well with the French, who I'd always had a sneaking suspicion liked me more than they let on.

The idea that the president of the United States was at some level goading us to lose—Trump had advised me, in his Twitter meltdown, to "WIN first" before speaking up—united us and acted like fuel on the fire. There was no conditional tense, no "we hope to win" or "we'd like to win." No. We were going out there and we were fucking winning.

The following day, when we walked onto the pitch at Parc des Princes in front of forty-five thousand people, it felt as if the eyes of the world were upon us. Even in ordinary circumstances, the quarterfinal of a huge tournament can feel bigger than the final. If you win decisively in the quarters, it creates a momentum that can carry you all the way to the trophy. That the match was against France, the host nation, only added to the hugeness of the occasion. And after the week we'd had, the fact was we weren't just playing for the US. We were playing for diversity, democracy, inclusion. We were playing for the right to be different and to still be respected. We were playing for equal rights, equal pay, and the glory of the women's game. We were playing to make an argument that winning didn't mean stomping on anyone else, but doing everything you could to support them.

I wasn't energized by hate. Hate leaves me indifferent. In the aftermath of Trump's remarks, it was the outpouring of love, from the Americans and the French, that inspired me. It was patriotism, pure and simple, an expression of everything we held dear about our country that Trump had been desecrating. Inside the stadium, the temperature was 90 degrees. Outside, ticket scalpers were prowling, a rare occurrence in women's soccer. The whistle blew, the crowd roared. I emptied my mind of everything but the game.

They wanted to beat us so badly. When the French dig in, they are tough opponents, and this game wasn't going to be an easy ride. Five minutes in, Alex Morgan was fouled by Griedge Mbock Bathy, the French defender, and we won a free kick. I took it from about twenty-two yards out. The ball curved low, slicing through a crowd in the goal mouth that included Amandine Henry, the French captain, and our own Julie Ertz, before dropping down into the far right corner of the net. Sarah Bouhaddi, the French goalkeeper, barely had eyes on the ball. She couldn't do a thing to stop it.

I hadn't really planned what happened next. Once before, in a friendly, I had thrown my arms out after a goal and without giving it much thought, had it in my back pocket that day. After my goal, the noise, the thrill, and the sheer wave of joy from the crowd slammed into me with an almost physical force. That kind of energy requires space, and I threw open my arms—shit-eating grin, chest out, heart wide-open, staring defiantly up at the crowd: Are you not entertained?! It was simultaneously a moment of pure performance and an undiluted animal reflex. We are here; we are smiling; we are not going down.

Eight minutes later, Eugénie Le Sommer made a decent header that fell just wide of the net, caught expertly by our goalie, Alyssa Naeher. For the rest of the first half, the French seemed rattled, allowing Becky and Julie to dominate midfield. But early in the second half, after two great back-to-back saves by Bouhaddi, they started to come back.

For the first ten minutes, France had the edge and put us on the back foot. Then, twenty minutes into the second half, Alex passed a long ball up the field to Tobin, who found me on the left side, unmarked. In what seemed like an eternity, the ball trickled toward me and a second later, the net was shaking. Two–nil up! I screamed off the adrenaline, fists clenched, yelling into the crowd, then knuckled down and got back in the game. France wasn't done yet. In the eighty-first minute, Wendie Renard, the tallest player in the tournament, pulled off a spectacular header that sailed passed Naeher and brought the French to 2–1. It was a beautiful shot that for the French came too late. The whistle blew. The French collapsed. We were through.

As an athlete, rising to the moment and slamming home a win when you most need it feels like everything you were put on this planet to do. As a human being, it's just the beginning. The night we won against France was the eve of the Paris Pride march, which takes place at the end of LGBTQ Pride Month. In the post-game interviews, I talked about the match and the goals, then drew attention to the team itself. "You can't win a championship without gays on your team," I said to reporters. "Go gays!" We were happy, fabulous, and on every front page in the land. This is what winning for the United States looked like.

We had four days off before the semis against England and my phone wouldn't stop pinging. Half the messages were congratulations; the other half were concerns. From inside the World Cup bubble, I was shielded from a lot of the fallout from my spat with the president, but I understood from my messages it was still raging. The family text chain hadn't gone this wild since my mom stepped on the lid of a trash can and nearly decapitated herself. (She'd been fine; none of us could stop laughing.)

CeCé, at home in Redding, called me in a panic, and when her reception cut out, asked me to text her everything I was feeling and to reassure her I was OK. Rach, in France, rolled her eyes and couldn't believe I'd managed to upset everyone again, while she was still as always,

100 percent behind me; Jenny was worried about my safety. Sue, in the US with her team, wrote a whole article for **The Players' Tribune** backing me up ("So the President F*cking Hates My Girlfriend . . .") that swiftly went viral. Brian, at a rehab facility in San Diego, had been texting me encouragement throughout the tournament and told me he was totally in my corner.

My parents were in France, and while they were ecstatic after our quarterfinal win, they were anxious that the president's remarks put me in danger. All I could tell them was not to worry; nothing had happened in 2016, and nothing was going to happen now. The whole thing seemed completely ridiculous, besides which, we were way past the point of it making a difference. As every top athlete knows, you reach a point of pressure after which it simply can't get any higher. You can either use it to your advantage or go home.

I was nursing a minor hamstring injury after the quarters and couldn't play in the England game. England had done a great job against Norway, defeating them 3–0 with surgical precision in the quarters, and we knew we'd have a fight on our hands. Ten minutes into the match, before a packed stadium in Lyon, Tobin Heath ran down the right, passed to Kelley O'Hara, who made the perfect cross to Christen Press—1–0! Nine minutes later, England equalized. Before the halftime whistle went, Alex Morgan's header off a Lindsey Horan cross brought us up a goal and we finished the first half 2–1.

It was Alex's thirtieth birthday and she was feeling pretty jaunty. After her goal, she raised her pinkie in a gesture to imitate drinking tea and it was fucking epic. To tease the English is such a pleasure because they react immediately and get completely outraged. It was next-level trollery, provoking a ton of shit-talking from the English and sparking a whole new level of rivalry with Phil Neville's team, who are good, although not as good as Neville thinks they are. There was no harm, no foul, and the whole thing was pretty funny, not least because England suffered a major sense of humor failure. I couldn't blame them. After Alyssa Naeher saved a penalty kick in the eighty-fourth minute, they were out and we were into the final.

Four days later, we ran out in front of sixty thousand people in Lyon. We weren't complacent. We never are. But I think we expected to score against the Netherlands early on in the match, as we had in every other match in the tournament. Instead, it took us thirty-one minutes to even make a shot on goal. After I'd sent a corner kick to Julie Ertz, she flicked it toward the goal, to be deflected by Sari van Veenendaal, the Dutch goalkeeper, who staved off two shots from Alex in rapid succession. We were pressing hard and getting nowhere.

In the second half, a foul by Stefanie van der Gragt gave us a penalty kick and I stepped up. It's hard to describe how a moment like that feels. It's not that you block out the crowd. When sixty thousand people are screaming your name, you're aware that they're there. It's more like you take the noise and the energy and push it down into a blade of concentration, using it to intensify your power and skill. This was it—the chance to get ahead in the biggest World Cup final of our lives.

I took one short breath, ran at the ball, and smacked it cleanly with my right foot, directing it down the middle and slightly to the right of Van Veenendaal, then watched as it flew into the back of the net. In between running to the corner and being mobbed by the entire team, I managed to throw out my arms in what was now a signature pose. Eight minutes later, Rose Lavelle sprinted up the middle of the field, outrunning Van der Gragt and Anouk Dekker, and smashed in a goal that effectively finished the game. The Dutch never regrouped. We had won.

It can be hard to re-create, later on, the rush of a moment like that. You collapse. You cry. You jump on the backs of your teammates. Everything we were had rested on this win, and as Gianni Infantino, the FIFA president, awarded us the trophy, the crowd started chanting something it took a second to understand. "Equal pay!

Equal pay!" The words rang around the stadium as blue and gold confetti rained down, and Tobin dropped to the ground to make confetti angels. It was unbelievable. "It's ridiculous," I said, when a microphone was shoved into my face. I didn't know what else to say. For once, I was lost for words.

This was the fourth World Cup win for the US women's team. It was the second World Cup title of my career, and it felt like the first World Cup win that might lead from soccer to other kinds of victory. A few days later, on a beautiful summer day, thousands of people thronged the sidewalks of New York as we stood on an open-topped bus, drinking champagne and wearing T-shirts with the words WORLD CHAMPIONS emblazoned across them in gold. Ticker tape rained down as the crowd shouted, "Equal pay!" and we screamed it back at them.

This was not a subtle celebration. At one point, I took a sip of champagne, threw my arms wide, and shouted, "I deserve this!" It was a moment of performance, much like my antics on the field, but also an acknowledgment that you can take pride in yourself without undermining your team. Along with Alex Morgan, I had been the tournament's top scorer and had been awarded both the Golden Boot and the Golden Ball for outstanding player. Damn right I deserved this.

An hour later, I stood on the steps of City Hall

under a banner reading ONE NATION, ONE TEAM, and after being presented with the keys to the city by Bill de Blasio, the mayor of New York, I made a speech. I thanked my teammates, managers, coaches, chefs, medics, ground staff, media team, and all the people who had cheered us on from day one. I even thanked the head of the federation, Carlos Cordeiro, who was sitting slightly awkwardly behind me, with the team. He had, I said, supported us throughout the tournament, and I hoped would support us in our mission to be paid equally with the men. I told him it was OK to get booed; everyone in power gets booed. In a moment of heady largesse, I even admitted it was possible that some of my unrehearsed statements that year had been a little divisive, and told him I looked forward to holding his feet to the fire.

I asked those watching to look at our team; black, white, gay girls, straight girls. I asked them to look at their own communities and consider how they might take tiny steps to improve them. "We have to love more, hate less, listen more, talk less," I said. "This is everybody's responsibility." I hoped that people could take what inspired them about the World Cup and apply it to their own lives.

I was appealing to our country as a whole, but I also wanted to make a point about the right of each of us to fully live our own lives. There's a fallacy in America that acting for the common good means sacrificing the individual. Well, as a person of robust ego, I am here to tell you that life doesn't work like that. The interests of the individual aren't at odds with the collective. You can win for the team and still celebrate your own performance.

I believe this especially with regard to women, whose individual needs have long been overlooked in favor of—oh, the irony—the collective good of men. When I yelled, "I deserve this!" I was speaking for women who are told to be selfless, invisible, meek; to accept less money, less respect, fewer opportunities, less investment. Who are told to be grateful, uncomplaining. Who are discouraged from owning their victories or even seeking them out in the first place. You can share, and help, and be part of your community, and you can also stand tall and enjoy your success. No caveat, no apology. Arms out wide, claim your space.

17

FORWARD

Fame is strange. When I stood on the steps of City Hall that day in July, I wasn't saying anything I hadn't said before, or that anybody else hadn't said. But fame gives your words weight and now people were listening. It makes no sense. If you're a good person and you're standing up for the right thing, whether you made the penalty kick shouldn't matter. As an athlete, the entry price for having political views is winning. The better you play, the more you win, and the bigger your platform becomes. I had flown back from the World Cup into a white-hot flare of fame, and while I wasn't rushing to put out a perfume, I had every intention of using the spotlight.

A week after returning from France, I put on a suit and went on CNN to say what I hadn't been able to say during the tournament. When Anderson Cooper asked if I had a message for the president, I smiled briefly at the absurdity of the situation. Then I looked into the camera. "I would say that your message is excluding people. You're excluding me, you're excluding people who look like me. You're excluding people of color; you're excluding Americans that maybe support you. I think that we need to have a reckoning with the message . . . 'make America great again.' I think that you're harking back to an era that was not great for everyone. It might have been great for a few people, and maybe America is great for a few people right now, but it's not great for enough Americans in this world. . . . You have an incredible responsibility as the chief of this country to take care of every single person and you need to do better for everyone."

The attention during that first week was intense. I'd become used to a certain level of recognition, depending on where we were in the tournament schedule, but this was different. Every time I stepped out of the house, I was recognized. My hair—which, depending on what color I could grab when I remembered to re-dye it, veered between pink and a sort of light eggplant—made me highly visible. (I was too vain to wear a hat; I don't look good in hats.) In June, right after my comments about not going to the White House became public, my agents had had to hire extra security at their office after receiving threatening messages, and I was still getting a lot of hostile attention. Most people were polite to my face—the only negative comment I got was from a guy who approached me on the street in Seattle, said, "Congratulations, but I wish you would represent America better," and after I said, "I'm sorry you feel that way," zoomed off again. But I wasn't digging into the comments on Instagram anytime soon.

At the same time, the level of support was overwhelming. As we toured the country in August, playing friendlies and exhibition victory matches, a new energy greeted us. I sat out a lot of those games—I was burned out, and injured, and wanted to reboot in time for the Olympics the following year—but I would still run onto the field and yuk it up for the crowd. We played Portugal, Ireland, and Korea in quick succession, and every time, the crowds were spectacular. They were cheering us for being the best in the world, but they were also, we thought, cheering us for what we'd said and stood up for.

There was a fun side to fame. I was invited to appear in a campaign for a fashion label, shoot a commercial, and go to a lot of parties. I bought myself that gold Rolex as a victory gift—no apology necessary—and shot a guest appearance on **The L Word**. When I was in my twenties, the TV show had been the only normalized representation of lesbians on-screen and an important part of my coming of age. Getting to appear on the show itself felt like arriving full circle.

My family got caught up in the excitement. Suddenly my mom was doing podcasts and my dad was being invited to do interviews on Fox News. "Dad!" I yelled down the phone. "You can't let Fox News into the house, they're doing takedowns of your daughter! Stick to local news!" (He never actually did the interview, although, god knows, Fox tried.)

I was bombarded with speaking offers. Even after the World Cup was a memory, I tried to say yes to everything that came in. I traveled the country, speaking to everyone from college kids, to women's and gay rights organizations, to payroll companies trying to navigate equal-pay claims. In airports and on the street, at matches and events, people came up to me and, after congratulating me for the World Cup win, invariably said, "You need to get paid." I was struck by how diverse they were—men, women, old, young, every ethnicity under the sun. "You get your money!" yelled a guy in the Philadelphia airport, and punched the air. The symbolism of being the best in the world and still being paid less than the men was so stark, so ridiculous. People, regardless of their background or their politics, were like: Oh, I get it.

To take advantage of this collective understanding of what we were fighting for, the Players
Association forged a partnership with Time's Up,
the advocacy group formed to address unequal
pay, sexual harassment, and other forms of gender discrimination in Hollywood and Beyond.
They'd had a tough time finding a vehicle for
their cause—actresses aren't a good reference
point for lots of people because, while they're
underpaid compared to male actors, they're still
paid a lot compared to everyone else. A partnership with us made sense.

In September, I won the Best FIFA Women's
Player of the Year award and flew to Milan for the
ceremony. Onstage, I spoke about how important it was to back one another up. I mentioned
Collin Martin, one of the few male soccer players
to have come out as gay, and Sahar Khodayari,
an Iranian woman who, after facing a prison
sentence for trying to watch a soccer match in a
country where women are largely banned from
being spectators, had killed herself before sen-
tencing.

I mentioned Raheem Sterling, the Manchester
City forward speaking out about racism in soccer. It wasn't enough to leave the antiracism campaign to him and other people of color, I said.
"I feel like if we really want to have meaningful change, everybody has to be outraged about

racism." This applied across the board. "If everybody was as outraged about homophobia as the LGBTQ players, if everybody was as outraged about equal pay or the lack of investment in the women's game as women—that would be the most inspiring thing to me."

I felt optimistic that fall. Just looking at the younger players on the team—the twenty-year-olds like Tierna Davidson who didn't need to come out, because they'd never been in—was very cool. All around us, young people were campaigning for change. When I looked at Greta Thunberg, or the kids from Parkland speaking out about gun reform, I saw a sense of urgency and responsibility to do something—anything— that I hadn't had at their age. At fifteen years old, they were where I was when I was thirty. They were leading the world.

In October, Jill retired. She'd won the Best FIFA Women's Coach Award at the same time I'd won Best FIFA Women's Player of the Year. Winning makes people generous, and while it was safe to say we weren't going to miss each other, the parting speeches were civil. The new coach, Vlatko Andonovski, had been at Seattle Reign since Laura left in 2018 and was known and trusted. At the end of the year, as the season wound down, the team looked toward Tokyo

2020 and the one goal that had eluded us: nailing Olympic gold after winning a World Cup.

It would have been easy to float through the holiday season picking up awards and drinking champagne. I liked the red carpet. I liked meeting people and doing fashion shoots; suddenly my theatrical side had a whole new outlet. The tricky thing was figuring out how best to use the attention. I was having a good time, but I didn't want to let myself, or the people using me for content, lose sight of why we were there.

In November, I accepted an award from **Glamour** magazine at a big celebrity ceremony in New York. It was a tough speech to write and I worked on it with Jess, who was always a great help when I needed to clarify my thoughts. I was grateful for the award and the platform it gave me, but I was also wary of self-congratulation. As we worked on the speech, Jess and I talked about who would be in the audience—powerful people with large platforms and followings. When addressing this crowd, I felt I needed to acknowledge just how privileged we all were.

The night was freezing cold. We arrived at the ceremony and walked into a venue packed with Hollywood stars. When I gave my speech, even before I thanked my mom, who was in the audience, I thanked the person who had started all this—Colin Kaepernick. Were it not for his bravery, I wouldn't have been standing there at

all, and I couldn't be at an event at which powerful people celebrated one another without pointing out the discrepancy in our experiences. While
I was enjoying the best year of my career, Colin
was still out of a job. We'd said and highlighted
the same things about racism, but he was out and
I was in. You do the math.

I went through the list of people whose activism had enabled my own: Tarana Burke, who
founded the Me Too movement; the community
organizers Patrisse Khan-Cullors, Alicia Garza,
and Opal Tometi of Black Lives Matter. I mentioned Gloria Steinem and Audre Lorde, and
recognized those such as Trayvon Martin and
Sandra Bland, whose deaths had swung a spotlight on how pervasive racism still is. I urged
those present to use their power to lift others up,
to throw down the ladder and extend their privilege. This meant being honest with themselves.
Everyone in the room was great at their jobs, but
that wasn't the only reason why many of us were
there. "I'm not going to act like my whiteness has
nothing to do with me standing before you now,"
I said.

I am still amazed at how many people didn't
get this. You have to be patient, people said; you
have to wait for everyone to get on the same page
as you. To which I say: Do we? Really? I don't
think basic human rights need to take time.

Politics and sport don't mix was the other comment I heard; and while I understood that for lots of people sports are an escape from real life, I didn't really care. Racism, sexism, and pay inequality are all pressing issues, and god forbid someone should get you to think about them on your precious sports Sunday. People want to stay asleep and say, Oh, I don't understand what's going on. Well, read a fucking article. Becoming aware of what is happening in our world isn't difficult.

In December, I won the Ballon d'Or, the most prestigious award in the soccer world. Before the ceremony, I did an interview with the French organizers, calling on stars of the men's game—including Lionel Messi, Cristiano Ronaldo, and Zlatan Ibrahimović—to speak out against racism and sexism, and querying why they were so reluctant to do so. "Do they fear losing everything?" I said. "They believe that, but it's not true. Who will erase Messi or Ronaldo from world football history for a statement against racism or sexism?" I understood people were scared of losing their livelihoods. But when it came to stars of that magnitude, with that kind of wealth and power, fear of blowback just wasn't an adequate excuse.

There was one final award that year. Just before the holidays, I was named the **Sports Illustrated** Sportsperson of the Year. This was a big deal. The award has been around since the 1950s and previous winners included Muhammad Ali, Michael Jordan, and Tiger Woods. The glitzy ceremony was in a hotel ballroom in New York, and after getting up onstage to receive the award, I said a few things about the magazine. Was I really, I asked, only the fourth woman in the award's sixty-six-year history who deserved to win? I didn't think so, just as it seemed unlikely that the only people qualified to write for the magazine were white men.

"Is it true," I said, "that so few writers of color deserve to be featured in this publication? No. Is it true that so few women's voices deserve to be heard and deserve to be read in this publication? I don't think so."

I know the speech raised a few eyebrows, since criticizing one's hosts isn't exactly considered polite. Even my agents cringed when I called the magazine out for racism and sexism while the editor sat ten feet from the stage. But I didn't give the award to myself or invite myself to the ceremony. Those in charge at **Sports Illustrated** were honoring me for my activism and shouldn't have been surprised. When I made those remarks, I was thinking about Jenny Vrentas, the reporter who'd written the magazine's cover story about me and was a woman in a job that is overwhelmingly white and male. According to the Women's Media Center, 90 percent of all bylines in sports reporting are men's. I was thinking about Colin Kaepernick, who was out of a job. That's who I cared about, not the CEO of **Sports Illustrated**.

This attitude baffles some people, I know. I've heard the phrase "bite the hand that feeds you," which makes me laugh; I don't think of any hand as feeding me. And I don't need permission from an awards panel to speak my mind. If any permission is needed, it comes from my family, who raised me to be open and honest, and who gave me a good sense of whom to trust. When I say something "rude," I think about who I am saying it for, not who I am saying it to. By the time I get into a room with US Soccer, or **Sports Illustrated**, or the FIFA president, or a bunch of Hollywood stars, I am sure enough of my position to not sweat the reception. I don't need them to like me to know I am right.

Of course I had doubts, and I asked myself if any of this is actually effective. Am I doing enough? Or am I just talking, talking, talking? I wanted to put my platform to good use, but I didn't want to be the person who takes the microphone from somebody with less access and a different experience. It had been an incredible year, during which I had won so much praise for speaking out that it was frankly becoming uncomfortable. The only way to overcome this unease was to push harder. But in the absence of tangible results, it could be difficult to measure the impact.

Occasionally I would hear something that made me think my message was getting through. Earlier in the year, my aunt Wendy, my mom's sister, who had worked for several years as a program coordinator at a university, had been offered a promotion. What I found out later was that the university had wanted her to take the job, which entailed a lot of new responsibilities, without a pay raise, even though her salary had been frozen for three years. They would never have done it to a man, she thought, and told them she couldn't take the job without more money. In response, they dissolved her position.

Weeks after the fact, I learned from Wendy that the reason she'd asked for the pay raise—the first time she'd done so in her career—was because of the noise around the national team lawsuit. "It's not just a campaign for young people," she said. "I'm in my sixties and it resonated with me—equal pay and equal conditions for women. I took a risk and it didn't work out, but it was worth it." That they'd fired her was shocking. But sticking up for herself and asserting her worth had delivered another reward. "People are saying things are so much better than they were," said my aunt from the hospital bed where she was receiving treatment for cancer. "But let's go beyond better."

In December, ahead of the Democratic presidential primaries, I endorsed Elizabeth Warren for president. I found her phenomenal, a great communicator, totally relatable, and super smart. She was hitting it out of the park along the campaign trail and was highly organized, with great policies that were bold enough to not follow the moderate line. On a video call, I told her she had my vote and repeated a saying we had on the national team: LFG (the polite version of it: Let's go).

At the end of December, the whole team flew to Miami for the wedding of my teammates Ali Krieger and Ashlyn Harris. The event was beautiful, a totally over-the-top wedding that was covered in the pages of **People**. To have that level of mainstream publicity and excitement for a lesbian wedding felt like a genuine line in the sand, as did the fact that they had a traditional ceremony. I've always been annoyed when people say, "Oh, gay couples can do whatever they want for their weddings," implying that our weddings are totally different. There's only so many ways you can rejig an event like that, and most of us don't want to reinvent the wheel. Make no mistake— Ali and Ashlyn's wedding was very gay indeed; but their "normal" ceremony was a sign of how far we'd come.

I had to refocus, heading into the new year, and get back to peak levels of fitness. I had played a light season after the World Cup; now was the time to knuckle down and get serious. In January 2020, we flew around the country for the Olympic qualifying tournament, which we won for the fifth time in a row (highest scoring game: 8–0 against Panama). In the spring, however, my game really started coming together. Looking ahead to the Olympics that summer, I felt the first surge of adrenaline.

It might be considered a strange coincidence that, once again, we would be playing a major tournament with a pay dispute hanging over our heads—but we'd been arguing with the federation about pay for so long, the situation had simply become the new norm. Our lawsuit was ongoing, and we had a court date scheduled for May 5. Most of us assumed that the case would be resolved before then. Going to court would be time-consuming and expensive for everyone involved, but beyond that, we believed US Soccer would seek to avoid what would be a PR disaster. Looking back to the previous summer, when we had stood on the steps of City Hall and felt the world cheering us on, most of us believed our case had been made. Surely the federation could see that.

In February, we flew to Florida for the start of our last big warm-up before the Olympics, the SheBelieves Cup. With no settlement in sight and the federation's position still a mile from our own, we wore our warm-up shirts inside out as an act of protest. At least no one could accuse us of being distracted. Our dominance at the World Cup had, once and for all, put to bed the lie that campaigning for a cause compromised our performance. When that cause was asking our bosses for the respect we deserved, there was no greater incentive on earth.

Our first game of the tournament was against England. I stepped onto the field and felt a familiar sensation. It went all the way back, through three World Cups and two Olympic Games, to being six years old and running around for the Mavericks. I felt the give and bounce of the grass beneath my feet. I felt the sun on my back, as a million muscle memories twitched into action. I didn't know exactly what was coming, but whatever it was, I knew I had the instinct, training, and ability to react. We won the game, and the game after that, and then faced Japan in the final. Seven minutes in, I stepped up for a penalty, launched it over the huddle of Japanese players in the goal mouth, and watched as it arced over the goalkeeper to the back of the net. It didn't matter how many times it happened. There was no feeling like it.

Ten days later I was back in New York. It was March 13, 2020. There was still no settlement from the federation; quite the opposite, in fact. A few days earlier, our bosses had released a statement arguing that physical differences between men and women meant that not only did we have less "ability," "skill," "speed," and "strength" than the men, but that being a male player "carries more responsibility within US Soccer" than the women's team does.

You'd think we'd be used to these sorts of comments. You'd think there would be nothing they could say at this point that would surprise us. But even by the standards of the federation, their words were bald-faced misogyny, and, for a second, we were shocked. There was an instant, massive outcry, and US Soccer hastily backed down. But it was too late, and as our shock subsided, it turned to something more like glee. My god, they had said out loud what they had always been thinking. We see you now, we thought. The whole world sees you now.

All we could do—all we could ever do—was go through the numbers again. Number one in the world. Winner of four Women's World Cup titles and four Olympic gold medals. Generator of $50.8 million in revenue between 2016 and 2018, and, a year later, winners of a World Cup final watched by 1.12 billion people. Most goals in a single Women's World Cup match. Most consecutive World Cup tournament wins. Winner of eight CONCACAF Gold Cups, ten Algarve

Cups, and seven Four Nations Tournaments. On and on it went.

After a few meetings in the city that day, I was due to meet up with Sue in Connecticut. It was a chilly afternoon, overcast with sudden gusts of wind. The streets should have been full with Friday afternoon rush hour traffic, but as the car drove me through Manhattan, everything was quiet. Three days later, in response to COVID-19, the New York City public school system closed. A few days after that, the whole city shut down, as did most of the country. As I crossed the Henry Hudson Bridge and traveled on through the Bronx, I thought ahead to the coming months. The federation would give us a deal. We would win at the Tokyo Olympics. Perhaps by Christmas, we would even have a new president. To win, you have to believe it will happen. After that, it's just a question of being bolder, braver, more inclined to speak up, and—in any way you can—better.

EPILOGUE

When I knelt during the anthem in 2016, I had no end goal in mind. It was a reflex born of solidarity with Colin and my experiences as a gay woman in a straight, male-dominated world. I wanted to broaden the conversation about racial injustice and to support a fellow athlete. And while I hoped it might encourage others to act, if it didn't, I would continue to do it anyway.

Four years later, we are in a new world. In June 2020, in the wake of the death of George Floyd, a forty-six-year-old black man killed by a police officer in Minnesota in May, we are seeing scenes that would have been inconceivable a year ago. Across the country and the world, people are marching in protest against racial injustice. Demonstrators are gathering in LA and Oakland, in Washington, DC, and Muncie, Indiana. By mid-June, at least 1,700 demonstrations across all 50 states have taken place. In Paris, Milan, and Berlin, meanwhile, protesters hold up signs reading JUSTICE CAN'T WAIT, while in Britain, the entire Liverpool soccer squad takes a knee. Colin Kaepernick's symbolic act, for which he paid such a price, is a global movement.

For months, as the pandemic rages, the world has been living under lockdown. In America, the spread of the coronavirus has revealed the system for what it is, laying bare the lie—for anyone who still believes it—that this country works for the majority of people. Alongside millions of uninsured for whom having no health care is commonplace, 40 million people have filed unemployment claims and seen their health care evaporate with their jobs.

For those millions of parents suddenly homeschooling their kids, it is glaringly obvious that we need to pay teachers more. And after it comes to light that over a third of deaths from COVID-19 are nursing-home residents and workers, it is clear we need to take better care of our elderly.

There are other lessons. When small business loans are scooped up by big companies, it is a reminder not only that society favors the rich, but also that we have our priorities wrong. While the people we've been told are important stay home, the undervalued and ignored—supermarket and health care workers, technicians, delivery workers, people who clean the hospitals and take the bodies to the morgues; people of color, women, immigrants, undocumented people—have literally been deemed essential.

Sue and I ride out the pandemic at our apartment in Connecticut. The Tokyo Olympics are postponed, possibly forever. I spend the mornings working out and the afternoons engaging with activists and politicians. I connect with Patrisse Cullors, one of the cofounders of Black Lives Matters. I speak with Joe Biden and Alexandria Ocasio-Cortez. I have a conversation with Gavin Newsom, the governor of California. We speak about how to get through this together, how policy and activism might meet, and about the failings of the person in the White House. We could have had $2 trillion more to put into the economy if the president hadn't given it away in a tax cut. The cost of his fumbling response to the pandemic can be measured in the tens of thousands of lives, the brunt of them from communities of color.

It is bigger than Trump. The pandemic and the national uprisings are a once-in-a-many-generation opportunity to look at what we consider important, to reimagine who we are and want to be. After months of lockdown, the swell of protests in the wake of the deaths of George Floyd, Breonna Taylor, Ahmaud Arbery, and so many others seems to provide an obvious answer. We want to be better. We want to look beyond ourselves to others who are hurting. After months of staying inside to flatten the curve and shield the most vulnerable, most of us understand that only by acting in one another's interests might we fully protect our own. When, in early May, a judge rejected my team's pay equity claims (we immediately appealed), the men's national team stepped up and spoke in our defense. A month later, the NFL lifted its ban on kneeling during the anthem. A week after that, the US Soccer Federation did the same.

Real change lies within all of us. It is in the choices we make every day. It's in how we talk, who we hire, and what we permit others to say in our presence. It's in reading more, thinking more, considering a different perspective. At it's simplest, it's in whether we're willing to spend even five minutes a day thinking about how we can make the world better. By the time you have this book in your hands, four months from now, I have no idea what the world will look like. But I do know that in a country where years, decades, centuries can go by in which things carry on pretty much as before, the uncertainty thrills me and gives me hope. Everything is changing. It's happening now. And it's just the beginning.

Let's go—really, let's go.

Acknowledgments

To Jessica Clarendon, without you none of this would be possible. For so long, you have been and continue to be my north star. For the hours spent listening to me rant, listening to me struggle, listening to me learn, all the while challenging, guiding, and educating me at every step, thank you. I promise to never put you on a boat in the Hudson again, but then again, I might. I look forward to all the "Good Trouble" we will continue to get ourselves into. MRS.

I spent hours on the phone with Emma Brockes—hours in person, on text, and over email. She spent hours with my family in Redding, talking with Sue, and talking with my friends and teammates. I never could have imagined the beautiful story you would weave together. It was a mirror to things seen and unseen, spoken and not—a journey through the heart and mind of a little girl from a small town with a wild family and a big dream.

I have known Dan Levy since I was barely an adult. He has been such a rock throughout my career and my life no matter what, always standing right with me, guiding me, and giving it to me straight. (Dan was supportive of the pink hair from the beginning, FYI.) I can't thank you enough.

I do not say this lightly or with hyperbole: the first time I ever felt truly seen—for all I had done and all I had the potential to do, for the woman I was and could become, all my flaws, all my whole damn self—was in a Brooklyn conference room with a beautiful view of the Brooklyn Bridge, when Ann Godoff walked in. I will never forget it. Ann, you changed my life. Thank you.

To all my teammates over the years, too many to name: a simple thank you. Every one of you encouraged me to be myself and loved me for who I was, which, to me, is the greatest gift.

And to all the LGBTQIA+ kids out there: I see you, I hear you, I love you, and with every breath I have I will fight for you. You are beautiful.

Megan Rapinoe is an American professional soccer player. As a member of the US Women's National Team, she helped win the 2015 and 2019 FIFA Women's World Cup tournaments and a gold medal at the 2012 London Olympics. A cocaptain of the team since 2018, she was named the Best FIFA Women's Player in 2019 and was awarded the Golden Boot.